THE FIGHT FOR BRISTOL

D1419808

Cover illustration: Lodge Street, Bristol

THE FIGHT FOR BRISTOL

Planning and the growth of public protest

Editors
Gordon Priest
Pamela Cobb

Contributors
Dorothy Brown
Patrick Brown
Pamela Cobb
Richard Flowerdew
Peter Floyd
Anne and Jerry Hicks
David Hirschmann
Gordon Priest
Reece Winstone

BRISTOL CIVIC SOCIETY
and
THE REDCLIFFE PRESS
BRISTOL

First published in 1980 by
Bristol Civic Society
and
Redcliffe Press Ltd
14 Dowry Square, Bristol 8

ISBN 0 905459 25 3

Printed in Great Britain by
BURLEIGH LTD
Bristol

Contents

*Dedicated with
grateful thanks
to the memory of
Jim Preston
and
John Totterdill*

Preface

Nineteen-eighty sees the 75th anniversary of the founding of the Bristol Civic Society. In 1965, it seemed appropriate to publish a slim volume recounting the society's first sixty years.

In a mere fifteen years since then the pace of redevelopment and the scale of public reaction to it has been such as to justify a more substantial record. Not only is there more to tell, there are many more groups and societies in the picture. This time it is fitting for the Civic Society to mark its own anniversary with an account of the wider scene.

However forward looking the amenity movement may hope to be it cannot forget its roots. The title under which the Civic Society first operated underlines this. The Bristol Kyrle Society was one of several which adopted the name of John Kyrle, who lived in Ross-on-Wye and died as long ago as 1724. He built a causeway, planted a wood and generally fostered his community in the paternalistic fashion natural to his time. Little of this would have been remembered if Alexander Pope had not heard of him and held him up under the name of 'The Man of Ross' to shame those wealthy landowners who hoarded as misers or spent vast sums on building and landscaping for their own aggrandisement rather than the public good.

Happily for us, we can now enjoy many of the stately homes built by Pope's contemporaries but like him we cannot approve current developments which do not have a strong social content. The pages of this book amply testify to this commitment. John Kyrle is still a valid symbol for the amenity movement.

Jack Miles
President, Bristol Civic Society   **May 1980**

Introduction

Local democracy has always been a strong point of the British system. The power of Whitehall has been continuously eroded by local communities on matters having a direct impact on local affairs. With municipal governments growing into bureaucratic machines in order to cope with the complex problems of modern society, the rise of powerful pressure groups outside government has allowed the operation of real democracy beyond the ballot box.

The history of post-1945 planning provides a remarkable instance of this. At the end of the war there was an all-pervading mood for a clean sweep of everything tawdry, dirty and inefficient in our badly damaged cities. Central government responded to this mood, setting up, through the Planning Acts, a structure that gave local authorities immense powers to control and direct the physical environment.

But the dream of a brave new world was not achieved. Town planners, administrators and architects were not up to the challenge. Often, they were frustrated by institutional resistance to change; conservatism about the new architecture and fears of draconian land acquisition powers meant that most plans, when finally ready for implementation, were thin shadows of the original dreams. The new planning structure, devised to create a new Britain, resulted in charmless environments that replaced ones that many people began to remember with affection.

The growth of the amenity society movement since the war reflects the growth of disillusion with the dream. This book sets out to illustrate this development by examining examples in the city of Bristol and by showing how a local community fought not only against insensitive planning but against what increasingly was seen as the undemocratic character of the planning system.

The rapid growth of the amenity movement has been accompanied by a remarkable change in the relationship between amenity societies and politicians and professional planners. Again using Bristol examples, this book looks at the changing relationships between planners and public.

The first section traces the background – the problems facing the city planners at the end of the war, and how they tackled them; there follows a description of the beginnings of protest and the formation of new amenity societies. The second section is devoted to 'case studies': the Outer Circuit Road, the Avon Gorge and the Grand Spa Hotel, Kingsdown and the Hospital Board, and the City Docks. The third section is concerned with the changes in attitude in the 1970s as the amenity societies grew stronger and more positive: new uses for old buildings, urban renewal, conservation programmes, and open spaces, trees and woodlands.

During the period under review, there have been fundamental changes in attitudes to planning and architecture. It is too soon for a measured assessment of those changes and this book does not attempt one. What it does is to record in a permanent form some part of what actually happened. The record has been compiled by some who took part on the amenity movement side and it may therefore be biased, though the contributors and the editors have attempted to produce a balanced story.

PART I

BACKGROUND

Setting the scene. Planning in Bristol since 1945

Bristol emerged from the Second World War with large areas in ruins. Thousands of homes, and many historic buildings, had been destroyed or damaged by Hitler's bombs. Apart from the appalling loss of life, the greatest tragedy of the war in Bristol was the total obliteration of the city's ancient shopping area. Whole streets, from Wine Street to Castle Street in the east and to Bristol Bridge in the south, were reduced, in one night, to a mass of rubble and twisted girders. The disappearance of familiar landmarks – the medieval St. Peter's Hospital, the black and white timbered Old Dutch House, and many others – was especially grievous and disorienting.

With the end of war in sight, a 'Reconstruction Committee' was set up in 1944 to preside over a major rebuilding programme. The refashioning of the city centre, the clearance of sub-standard housing and the provision of new, were urgently required.

Even before the war, Bristol's City Engineer held the title of Planning Officer, too – an unusual situation then. The Bristol and Bath Regional Planning Scheme of 1928, prepared by Sir Patrick Abercrombie for a group of local authorities, was an impressive initiative taken without government backing. It did not produce much on the ground but has affected planning philosophy with its ring road systems right up to the present day.

The post war period produced a new social awareness and a government determined to create radical legislation. The Town and Country Planning Act, 1947, was a key part of this, requiring cities to produce plans and take on the control of land use and all new development.

There was an immediate need for planning departments and planning officers. The Town Planning Institute at that time was small and there were simply not enough planners to go round. Members of other professions returning from the war were offered crash courses and men from widely differing backgrounds, after years in uniform, again found themselves fighting but this time to get the City moving.

In Bristol, the City Architect dealt with the vast council housing programmes for the Housing Department together with matters of aesthetic concern, particularly the City Centre. The City Valuer controlled the letting and development of the extensive city estates including large parts of the central area. The City Engineer provided the roads, drains and services needed for these schemes. The City Planning Officer, working closely with the Engineer, fulfilled his new statutory functions in the production of the Development Plan and in controlling development.

In 1952, the first Development Plan was published; it covered a twenty year period and was to be reviewed every five years. It foresaw a greatly improved city. There were to be new housing estates on the outskirts, to replace the sub-standard early housing being cleared in the central areas, based on neighbourhoods of 50,000 population. Since the private car was a rarity, local shops, schools, churches would be provided for each community. Jobs were to be created on new trading estates especially designed to accommodate heavy lorries away from housing areas; main roads were to be widened and improved. In the Centre, bomb damage clearance, the rebuilding of the shopping area and completion of the Inner Circuit Road, which had started before the war, were urgent priorities. Radical and controversial decisions were taken to resite the shopping area in Broadmead – a more spacious site – and to create a new Civic Centre at Wine Street.

New ideas were being discussed all over the country. At Coventry, Exeter and Plymouth nothing had yet begun. The talk was of multi-levels, roof top parking, pedestrian malls and rear servicing. Alternative schemes were proposed but speed was of the essence. The roads were there and were adequate. The land was acquired, compulsorily if necessary. Some historic buildings were kept and rear servicing provided but if the developers were to be attracted there must be vehicles at the front door and not too much control, although the City Architect did require uniform building

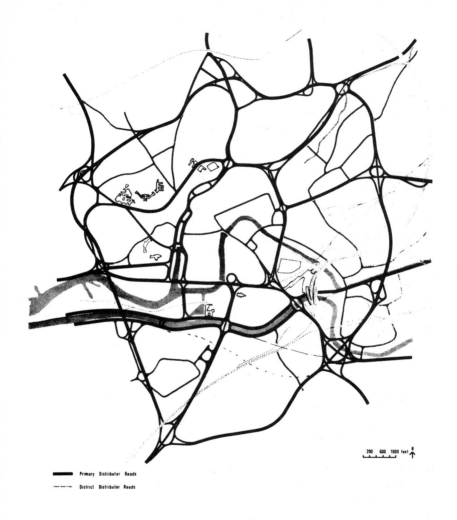

Primary Distributor Roads
District Distributor Roads

The Inner and Outer Circuit Roads from the 1966 City Centre Policy Report.
A planners' dream thwarted by public protest.

13

Prewar bustle in Castle Street; the barrenness of its replacement in Broadmead has only recently been softened by landscaping and pedestrianisation.

heights and materials after the first few buildings had caused complaint.

But by the early 1960s, the central area was still in ruins. Except for Broadmead, nothing had happened. The proposed Civic Centre at Wine Street failed to materialise. Old Market Street and the Tramway Centre had diminished in commercial and social significance. The city did not appear to have a heart any more. In the event, Broadmead both because of its location and because of its architectural qualities, failed to provide the new focus that the planners had anticipated.

The post war dreams of a brave new world began to fade and protests and alternative views on the development of the city began to be heard. A new concept was needed.

The Architects' Forum, a group of young Bristol architects, produced their Plan for Bristol in 1961. It was for a twentieth century city based on a free flow traffic design of a type already common in Germany and America before the war and it suggested the vertical segregation of vehicles and pedestrians particularly on the Centre.

Bristol's traffic engineers had built roads. A new section was now set up to design highways. The section produced a dramatic new plan with large roads to free flow standards by 1964 which was based on what it was felt the City would need, having surveyed and projected the massive growth in the use of the private car then occurring, rather than what the City could afford.

Following the Forum Plan, the Wine Street Campaign and other protests, the Planning Department employed their first architect/planners to investigate the design of the City Centre. From 1962 comprehensive redevelopment plans were produced, first for the St. Mary Redcliffe area, then the Lewins Mead area and later for the suburban centres. The schemes were essentially three-dimensional rather than social or economic and required the close co-operation of planners and developers.

By 1964, work was in hand for the first Review of the Development Plan which was published in 1966. It incorporated the already completed free flow road plans backed up by traffic surveys and projections for the future based on the routes already drawn which tended to show that even with such a massive road construction programme, future vehicular demand could not be satisfied.

The City Centre Policy Report, a large and detailed document, produced in advance of new government thinking, covered all aspects of work in the City Centre, and co-ordinated the separate schemes and policies already in hand, including the pedestrianisation of Broadmead, widespread pedestrian/vehicular segregation and massive redevelopment in an attempt to put the City Centre back together in a manner suitable for a modern city in the late twentieth century.

With a buoyant economy, sites were cleared and work progressed at speed. Lewins Mead and other areas scattered throughout the Centre were being redeveloped and plans drawn up. Kingsdown was cleared, Brunswick and Portland Squares and Victoria Street were all being considered.

The 1967 proposal to close the City Docks because they were no longer economically viable radically affected many of the most important proposals in the Development Plan Review. The Act of Parliament required to bring this about offered a new route via a floated cut for small boats only through new locks. This would have left part of the old Floating Harbour available to be filled in for redevelopment. Public opposition to the proposed dock closure, to the large and expensive road schemes and to the massive clearances of property was strong, vocal and increasingly well-organised. At the same time – by the late 1960s – the tower block products of the rebuilding were starting to appear on the city skyline. Much loved old buildings disappeared or were left empty. The environmental battles of the early 1960s had been heeded but the 'machine' had once again mangled the results. There were derelict sites everywhere. The new buildings were inhuman, huge and ugly and the roads destroyed the communities they were built to serve.

Local Government reorganisation in 1974 created two layers of planning. Bristol, proud City and County for six hundred years, was divested of its wider planning powers and the new County of Avon found itself in charge of five districts, one of which, Bristol, accounted for half the total population. The two authorities clashed frequently, with opposing political parties in power. Avon set about its task of producing a Structure Plan for the County as a whole, whilst Bristol District continued with its role of development control and local plans. At the time of writing, the Structure Plan is yet to be published but the interim policies produced by both authorities almost as soon as they were set up reflected the disillusionment felt at the destruction and development caused by the boom of the late 1960s and early 1970s.

Since, by 1975, the development market had collapsed and local government spending was being cut, both authorities were fairly safe in producing policies restricting further commercial development and road building.

During the 1960s and 1970s the amenity movement had gained strength and expertise. It had broadened its base from a few scattered groups to strong representation across wide areas of the city with some groups seeking to cover the city as a whole. Pressure from government to involve the public in decision-making through such agencies as Conservation Advisory Panels, together with greater expertise on the part of both the local authorities and amenity groups led, in the 1970s, to a degree of co-operation which contrasted sharply with the misunderstanding and mistrust of the previous two decades.

The 1960s: The need for protest

The 1960s was the decade of the motor car with plans being made, and sometimes executed, for great concrete routes through the hearts of our cities. Eighteenth and nineteenth century houses, designated slums, were cleared to make way for the new routes and for multi-storey car parks. The old amenity societies, and the new ones which sprang into existence in response to specific threats, called through the developing concrete jungles with uncertain voices. They were not listened to; nor, at first, were they certain themselves what they wanted to say. More or less everyone believed that the advancing tide of motor cars was inevitable: necessary, indeed, to the advance of civilisation. In the beginning, the amenity lobby could often be seen calling for more *radical* solutions to traffic flow problems than those advocated by the corps of borough engineers.

In Bristol this phase was demonstrated, in 1961, by the Forum Plan for Bristol. The group of architects who put it forward combined super highways with dreaming notions of pedestrian decks to create squares of Venetian splendour where Bristolians would gather in their thousands on election nights six metres above the smoothly uninterrupted flows of traffic. The dream seemed so achievable. Perhaps parts of it, at least, should have been done. The centre deck might have worked; noise and fumes might not have made it unusable. Often the wrong parts were carried out. The major central area civic contribution of the sixties was the complex of pedestrian decks that survive in truncated form above the street at Lewins Mead and beyond and which virtually nobody uses. This was to be the essential link between the Centre – or even Forum's great piazza above it – and the Broadmead shopping centre and beyond.

Early in the sixties, news from America began to filter through. Free flow for cars through city centres created more problems than it solved. The dream began to blur. If the private car and its keeper wanted free access to downtown, the roads and their

18

junctions would fill the whole town centre. Those urban freeways already built were making 'downtown' more and more undesirable. 'Easy in' meant 'easy out'. The effect was explosive. Firms, traditionally concentrated in the centre, moved to the green fields at the other ends of the freeways. American planners began to warn that the 'cure' was a killer. As local councillors and their planners in Britain lobbied and jostled to outdo each other in the scale of their urban motorways, the local civic societies, with examples from abroad, began belatedly to try to stop the flow. In cities like Bristol, the differences of view developed. There was little communication, let alone understanding, between the parties. The city, intent on building roads for which government money was available and which it believed were necessary both functionally and for reasons of prestige, displayed an almost total lack of sensitivity to the older fabric of the city.

A cavalier attitude to old buildings was not new in Bristol or elsewhere. The loss of buildings of quality and historic significance had been grievous, even in the not very vigorous economy before the war. After it, the losses caused by the war itself began to make people think about the worth of those old buildings that remained, but conservation was still a rare and surprisingly unremarked event. Although, also surprisingly, Bristol's boldest piece of post-war planning – the moving of the main shopping centre off the old castle hill onto the marshy flats of Broadmead – was accompanied by a number of conservation schemes, it also required the wholesale clearance of a down-at-heel, but virtually undamaged Georgian and seventeenth century area of considerable architectural quality. At least, the protection and re-use of the Greyhound Inn, Quakers' Friars, Lloyds Bank in Merchant Street, John Wesley's New Room and the Lower Arcade, mean that it remains an important place in Bristol's architectural heritage, albeit much reduced since the planners and developers started. Many important buildings were sacrificed in the fifties and sixties in the cause of progress. The voices calling against were muted. Bristol Civic Society was polite at first, believing that behind the scenes discussions were the right way to proceed. Today a level of mutual understanding has been achieved which permits dialogue between civic authority and civic society behind the scenes, but in the 1960s very great pressure was needed that had to be public if it was to be effective.

The Civic Society may sometimes have been too circumspect in dealing with the environmental crises of the sixties, but Bristol did not lack pressure groups ready and willing to speak firmly and publicly about the city's and the region's problems. Indeed, the early history of environmental pressure groups is well represented here. The Bristol and Gloucestershire Archaeological Society has existed since 1876 and has been active from the beginning of its career in urging the preservation of historic sites and buildings; much of this work was done at times when there were few planning or legal restraints on would-be destroyers. In 1912, the Society prepared a list of ancient monuments worth preserving for the Commissioners of Works and in 1921 it urged the Bishop of Bristol to set up an advisory committee on the preservation of the fabric and fittings of local churches.

In those days, members of the Society would carry out 'rescue digs' on threatened sites under their own initiative. Many important finds were made. In more recent times, the Society has played a full part in public local enquiries and is represented on the Conservation Advisory Panel.

The Council for the Preservation of Ancient Bristol was set up shortly before the Second World War and soon compiled a list of historic buildings in Bristol which, after amendment to take war losses into account, provided the basis in 1947 for the official lists compiled by the Ministry of Works. The Council has continued to maintain an active watch on preservation matters in the city.

In the 1940s an unusual local phenomenon emerged, where groups of activists appeared, either out of other organisations or around individuals, to promote specific projects and which then either dissolved or moved on to other projects or problems.

The first was a group of architects with plans to promote alternative proposals for the city which avoided relocating the city's shopping centre but which radically altered – indeed eliminated – the old street layout. This was in the middle and late 1940s when schemes were bold but perhaps a little unreal. A more recent manifestation of the same sort of *ad hoc* group prepared to work at a professional level to produce a cogent and usable plan to resolve a civic problem was the Bristol City Docks Group. Its members produced a massive and amazingly comprehensive set of reports and ideas at a time when the future of the City Docks was very much in the balance and when the local authority was divided and confused about what it should do with its 175 acres of obsolescent docklands.

Between these two lay twenty-five years and many groups. The first was a côterie of architects too wild to be contained by the august Bristol Society of Architects. They generated three classic and pioneering projects. The first, in 1960, an exhibition called 'Our City', directed attention to slovenly housekeeping in the city's streets. Set up in the front hall of the City Museum it created instant furore and was transported across the road to that other civic institution, the Berkeley Café. Out of this little storm were to grow the two other and more important things. The first was a monthly feature article in the *Bristol Evening Post* called 'Isambard'. The architects were given complete freedom to discuss Bristol architectural and planning issues. The group called itself Bristol Architects' Forum, an independent group within the Bristol & Somerset Society of Architects. The independence of the group was soon put to the test. Critical commentary on new Bristol buildings came as a complete shock to the Society and strenuous efforts were made to suppress the 'cuckoo'. Those were heady and exciting days. Never before (or since) did Bristol experience such a feast of polemic about the qualities of architecture and the social and political problems of urban design.

More important was the Forum's Bristol Plan. With Machiavellian skill, the Society of Architects, after failing to discipline the group, deflected their energies into 'something positive': the replanning of the Centre. The plan was detailed and radical. In an exhibition mounted at the Bristol Building Centre in 1961, it offered an only marginally idealistic planning solution for Bristol in the latter part of the twentieth century. The plan *was* traffic-oriented but not to the exclusion of people. A great deal of the group's energies were concentrated upon the problem of how to resolve the clash between people and cars. Thus appeared the Centre deck and re-routed radials to separate the neighbourhood

21

shopping zones from traffic arteries. This was in the days before Colin Buchanan's *Traffic in Towns*, but problems of environmental saturation were recognised.

The influence of the Forum Plan was enormous. Energetic young men and a very sympathetic local press introduced Bristolians to the notion that people outside the power structure could 'interfere' with decision-making. Out of Forum grew *Bristol Forum Journal* which survived for three issues, where problems like man and motors, the miseries of Bristol's suburban council housing, and the future of Ashton Court were discussed and argued.

After it came another literary milestone, *Output*, the occasional publication of The New Bristol Group. Even less remembered, perhaps, than *Forum*, its work was intended to be more political and directly influential in the corridors of power. It too achieved three issues. It covered subjects like housing in Bristol, general medical practice and health centres in Bristol, voluntary social service, Bristol's city art collections, University expansion, Bristol in partnership with its University, Bristol Zoo, Bristol 'preserved' and many more. Politicians were involved – usually rather left of centre, though it was meant to be non-party.

This period saw the first important environmental battle: the Wine Street Affair. This was a classic case, for it had all the characteristic features, with irreversible decisions taken against the spirit of previously published plans. What was unusual and unexpected was the strength of public response. The city, committed to a plan to form a new cultural heart to the city on the old shopping centre of Wine Street and Castle Street, quietly, in 1961, leased two key sites at the High Street boundary to an insurance company and the Bank of England with permission to develop, The amenity societies and others 'took to the streets'. For the first time, Bristolians were asked to comment. Ten thousand signatures were collected on a petition demanding that the City Council reverse its decisions to lease the land. The decisions were not reversed and the buildings were built, but no further leases were entered into and the future of the site as some sort of a civic one was assured.

The issue had been clouded by the production just previously of a remarkable little film made by a group centred around the

William Watts' shot tower was a notable casualty of road construction in the early 1960s, as was the remaining half of St. James' Square.

School of Architecture. The film was called *Dead Centre* and high-lighted the need to build up a rich mix of activities in city centres. It described Broadmead as the archetypal 'dead centre' – dead after 6 p.m. – and warned that the Wine Street/Castle Street proposals needed more than a museum and a park to make a real centre. It now of course has less than a museum. Perhaps even now, the citizens of Bristol should decide that, one day, Castle Park should accept buildings in and beside it that will convert it into the heart that Bristol still lacks.

Since Wine Street, the pace has changed and quickened and the impact of groups and societies has increased, though it is also true that some of the greatest environmental damage has been done. The destruction of Bristol's most important Georgian suburb in the 1960s was perhaps the worst of all the crimes committed in Bristol in the name of progress since the war. Almost all of Kingsdown still existed. Its destruction in the face of growing opposition is described later.

The second half of the 1960s was dominated by the great roads campaign. Some of the City's planners had been re-trained, appropriately via the University of Birmingham, to become traffic engineers.

One of the first major issues was the Downs Roundabout affair. In May 1961 the Bristol City Planning Committee had approved a scheme for a traffic roundabout on Durdham Downs beyond Blackboy Hill. The scheme was shelved the following January, but in September 1966 it was revived and approved. The scheme proposed a large roundabout to relieve traffic congestion at the expense of three and a half acres of Durdham Downs.

In 1966 there was a widespread feeling that traffic improvements were inevitable. Some might consider them an evil but there was no general feeling that they might often be unnecessary as well. But the encroachment on the Downs was another matter. In a letter to the *Evening Post* on September 17th 1966 the Chairman of the Civic Society launched a campaign against the scheme. By the time a petition was presented to the Council in November it had been signed by 13,394 people (an improvement on the 12,000 who signed the petition against the piecemeal development at Wine Street five years earlier).

A Public Inquiry was held in March 1967. There were in all 143 objections of which forty-one were heard at the Inquiry. Eighteen months later, the Minister approved the scheme. Then followed the gift by the University to the city of two and a half acres of land fronting Down House and the former Vice Chancellor's Lodge. This was included in the transfer of new land to make up for the loss occasioned by the roundabout scheme, which the Council was legally obliged to provide. The knowledge that the gift was imminent was described by a spokesman for the Planning Committee as the ace up their sleeves. However, this ace was trumped by the Minister of Housing who refused to accept the proposed transfer because it was margin land, already part of the Downs in all but a legal sense. The Council responded with a new plan revealed on June 17th 1970 which reduced the amount of land lost by including in the scheme the site of St. John's School which was due to move (as it did in 1979 although the building is still there, with proposals for its continued use).

In November 1973 it was observed that the roundabout scheme no longer appeared in any Highways programme. Like the Imperial Guard, the transport corps never surrenders but like old soldiers at least some of their schemes just fade away.

The City's Development Plan Review had to be subjected, as the law demanded, to public scrutiny. Allegedly quinquennial, it was five years overdue when it reached public inquiry in 1967. The Civic Society and the Bristol Society of Architects were the major opponents at the Inquiry. They mounted a fully professional case against many detailed aspects of the City's planning strategy and, most importantly, launched a detailed and carefully worked out argument against the real novelty in the plan – the proposal for an Outer Circuit Road. The multimillion road project might almost have been planned to mobilise opposition. The indicated route went through practically all the City's nineteenth century inner suburbs. Intersections were marked by blobs or sausage shapes that varied from drawing to drawing but which implied massive land area needs. There were to be bridges, tunnels and cuttings. The Civic Society's case, mounted with the help of a distinguished member of the Planning Bar, introduced reasoned academic assessment of planning processes using economists and social scientists as well as planners and architects as expert witnesses. As was usual in those days, the result of the Inquiry was not announced for several years. The announcement of the rejection of most of the objectors' argument did not come until 1970.

The Inquiry was the start of the longest and hardest fought environmental campaign waged in many parts of the City. More than any other this was a grass roots affair with planners and politicians doing battle with *real* people at public meetings. Today, there is no talk of an Outer Circuit Road except for the Glasgow-like fragment which churns through Easton to the City's shame and motorists' confusion. The scars are still there – at Totterdown, for instance, where a whole community and a lively neighbourhood went down before the bulldozers.

Totterdown residents are still in the battle. At the time of writing, Avon County Council is expected to bring road proposals to a Public Inquiry and the Totterdown Action Group with other amenity associations will be mounting a campaign.

The Review had been drawn up on the assumption that Bristol's City Docks would remain open, requiring massive engineering to bridge the harbour. The Civic Society challenged the need, being aware that the docks might well close. The proposed closure and the launching of the Bristol Docks Bill were announced a few weeks after the end of the Inquiry: a dramatic illustration of the secret non-participatory planning techniques of the time.

The Civic Society's detailed and careful approach in challenging the development plan at the Inquiry produced a new, independent pressure group. Realising that docks closure created the biggest single planning issue of the immediate future, some of the expert witnesses and lawyers involved in the Review Inquiry formed a group to study the planning problems of the area. Their work was published in 1968 as a booklet entitled *Bristol, the Central Area and its Waterways*. The group, which called itself the Bristol Planning Group, consisted of architects, civil engineers, economists, lawyers, operational researchers, town planners and statisticians. Its aim was 'to stimulate greater public discussion of planning problems in Bristol and to develop and encourage the use of thorough technical analysis to enlighten both discussion and decision-making in urban planning'.

The team contained a much wider range of skills than was then, or even now, available to the City's Planning Department. The aim of the publication was to demonstrate how new skills brought to bear on planning issues could allow alternative strategies to be drawn up and tested. It also introduced techniques for evaluating environmental factors. Through their techniques, the Group's members were able to show that land uses which seemed to be best financially were not necessarily so. Thus, the notion of allocating all the docks to office development and 'quick profit' in land deals would have massive hidden costs in terms of traffic needs and servicing. At the very time when the study was being carried out, the City was engaged in siting the vast new Polytechnic. The Planning Group's study demonstrated that, as a site for the Polytechnic, the City Docks would be economically viable and would have considerable environmental, as well as educational and social, advantages. However, although even hardened politicians warmed to the idea, there was no way in which the ponderous machine of local government could be deflected from the other site, at Coldharbour Lane outside the city.

By the end of the sixties, surprised and even shocked at the way that the people had responded to official attempts to create new urban dream worlds, government agencies had accepted the need for consultation. The Civic Trust, the Civic Amenities Act, Skeffington and others provided a new structure for the 1970s where planners and planned-for would live and work together for a somewhat modified ideal urban future.

At that very moment, a property boom engulfed the planners and the community. In Bristol, the boom held off long enough for the local authority and its planners to demonstrate that in any case they held no truck with the new wave. The extraordinary story of the struggle over the hotel in the Avon Gorge is told later in this book. This *cause célèbre* made a national impact and its public enquiry resulted in a positive change in the interpretation of planning law.

The Minister took the then unprecedented step of reversing an apparently final decision – was, both locally and nationally, a significant watershed. Since then, the amenity society movement has grown and has a new and significant role.

27

Buildings lost

The many *Bristol As It Was* titles by Mr. Reece Winstone constitute a visual record the like of which no other city in the country, perhaps in the world, can claim. Less well known is a simple list, also produced by Mr. Winstone, of 'changes in the face of Bristol'. Since 1960 he has kept a diary of changes for publication each year in cyclo-styled sheets. The changes are listed month by month. As he says, they are personal observations but they record virtually every important old building demolished in the years covered by the lists, together with all important new buildings built. The lists are not merely abstracted from newspapers but are the result of determined observation and continuous movement through the City. Mr. Winstone's aims were originally, 'with John Totterdill and other members of the Civic Society Committee, to tackle the problem of finding a twentieth century Latimer, but we had to admit failure. To continue the famous and unique *Annals of Bristol* from 1900 onwards where John Latimer left off proved an impossible ambition'.

There is no doubt however that between them, the books and lists provide an amazingly detailed record of Bristol's physical character in the nineteenth and twentieth centuries. Latimer's preoccupation was with social and political history. He only rarely commented on architecture. Mr. Winstone provides a superb record of the developing (or disintegrating) face of Bristol.

The list of buildings lost over the last two decades is indeed formidable, although the pace of demolition and the quality of buildings lost does definitely fall away as the 1970s advance. The 1960s started with a bang. The law library in the Guildhall in Small Street was altered by the City Architect and the last evidence of a Norman house of great splendour was destroyed. In 1961, good early or even pre-Georgian houses disappeared at such a rate that it is remarkable that any are now left. Vine Row and Old Park Hill went, complete with splendid shell hoods and panelled interiors, for University buildings. St. James's Parade

St. Andrew-the-less in Dowry Parade and all the buildings to its left were demolished in 1964 to be replaced by new flats. One of these, Lebeck House, contained fine panelled interiors and a splendid Georgian staircase.

went. Georgian cottages were removed without public outcry and Victorian commercial buildings like the *Western Daily Press* 'flat iron' in Baldwin Street and the splendid though mutilated Robinson building in Victoria Street were all cleared for progress.

The next year, 1962, started with the demolition of a complete, very slightly damaged redundant medieval church and tower, St. Augustine-the-Less, and ended with the demolition of the ruins of the Bishop's Palace in Anchor Road. The year saw whole streets demolished. In 1963 the pace slowed a little. A few important hillside houses on Granby Hill went as did a large and delightful area on the site of the Cumberland Basin flyover. Next year things speeded up again. Five houses in Prince Street, three in St. Thomas Street; Stokes Croft, Dowry Parade, Bridge Street, Henleaze Road – all lost Georgian buildings which were often of very high quality. Spendid Victorian monuments which went included the ruins of G. E. Street's All Saints, Clifton, the Harbour Master's House at Cumberland Basin, Gingell's great Victoria Street building which was latterly Henly's motor showroom and the Royal Exchange Building in Corn Street. The Hippodrome Tower was removed and the Empire Theatre demolished. Rownham House, Clevedale at Downend (Georgian mansions) and Brislington's seventeenth century Seven Gables were all demolished.

In 1965 houses were still being demolished on the Kingsdown hillside and in Stokes Croft. In the next two years the University demolished houses in St. Michael's Hill and the last part of the

Three losses in the 1960s and 1970s. Most of St. James' Parade demolished for offices; the ruins of the Bishop's Palace, burned in the Bristol Riots of 1831, cleared in 1963 for a new hall and gymnasium for the Cathedral School; St. Gabriel's Church, Easton, by J. C. Neale 1870, a splendid building needlessly destroyed.

30

great early eighteenth century square of St. James' with its shell hoods was pulled down to complete the Inner Circuit Road and much of Redcliffe Hill and the basically seventeenth century lead shot tower were cleared, again for road widening. By this time the pressure from the amenity societies was considerable but the planners seemed to be quite unstoppable. Traffic demands were still considered to be of prime importance to the prestige of the City, and in any case most of those traffic decisions had been taken years earlier.

In 1969 and 1970 the cluster of timber-framed houses at the bottom of Christmas Steps and in Narrow Lewins Mead were cleared to allow widening of the Inner Circuit Road, thus wiping out the last area of the centre of Bristol where one could stand entirely out of sight of any but eighteenth century or earlier buildings. A magnificent terra cotta bank in Temple Gate was sacrificed to progress in the form of a pedestrian bridge and an unattractive office block and the University demolished the Georgian building in Park Row where it started life; Paul Street, Kingsdown finally disappeared. In 1971, the famous Atlas and Sun Life Buildings on the Centre were replaced by slightly larger and much less attractive buildings. The ancient rectory of Temple Church which almost touched the tower was tidied into dust and a seventeenth century house in Clarence Road, St. Phillips, was destroyed. 1972 started and continued with the removal of many good Victorian commercial buildings in Victoria Street and Thomas Street, and Stokes Croft – one of the most ill-used streets in the centre – suffered a further loss with the removal of the Old Baptist College building.

The last few years, as Mr. Winstone's lists show, have suffered less but important buildings still go and others remain under threat. In 1973, some ancient and important gabled warehouses were pulled down on Broad Quay; in 1975, St. Gabriel's Church, Easton, was demolished in the face of great opposition and in 1978 The Garrick's Head on the Centre was pulled down. Much of what has gone was destroyed needlessly; all is irreplaceable. No amenity society should demand preservation at all costs but, with a civic record like Bristol's, it is not surprising that the city's societies seem more than usually sensitive to threats to old buildings.

31

The 1970s: The growth of the amenity movement

In the 1970s – the decade of lay involvement in planning – new local societies sprang up alongside the older ones and the specialist and national organisations. The important national legislation of the previous decade, making the participation of the ordinary members of the public in planning decisions a statutory obligation, began to take effect. In the 1960s, and to an extent now, societies like the Civic Society had architects active on their committees. Their presence has sometimes been thought to predispose them to decisions that seem to favour architectural or 'grand plan' notions; whether this is so or not, it is true that the new societies of the 1970s had fewer professionals and more lay people.

The newer societies discovered only slowly and with amazement the plans which had been adopted for the City. These involved the loss of hundreds of listed buildings. There was £400 million worth of road schemes, with multi-level junctions and throughways in all the inner city suburbs in a circle from Clifton to St. Paul's to Totterdown. All the radial roads were to be widened (some like Whiteladies Road still carry these widening lines). The Centre was to be redeveloped with tall blocks and to have four high-level pedestrian decks running like a succession of viaducts from one side to the other (rat runs as they were called). There was planning permission for a 300-foot high Post Office tower adjoining King Street (half as high again as, and four times the section of, the Bristol and West tower). Planning permission had been granted for millions of square feet of office blocks, without regard to possible future needs and implementation or the blighting effect on the city that the decisions created. Such plans obviously had their root in the optimism many people felt just after the war. Simply by starting again they could solve all modern problems. The plans produced by one professional group to rebuild the whole of the centre of the City seem incredible now.

By the end of the 1950s, some significant new things had happened. After decades when it was fashionable to move out of the city, the trend began to be reversed in favour of the neglected historic areas of Hotwells, Kingsdown and Clifton. Building societies preferred not to give mortgages on large old properties and it was Bristol City Council's admirably run and undiscriminating Mortgage Department which enabled the houses to be bought at all. Lovely and neglected Georgian houses were bought amazingly cheaply and began to be restored carefully. The people who moved in overlooked the central areas and started to take an interest in central area policies.

At the same time, the much-vaunted modern developments began to appear. The new Broadmead Shopping Centre was built, and people were appalled by its banality. The University buildings, dominating the skyline in the Centre, were a hideous disappointment. The repetitive lego of the speculative office builders set in seas of asphalt, began to demonstrate that modern wasn't better and that, if present policies continued, Bristol would shortly be a faceless city without character or history. In spite of the burgeoning movement back into the inner suburbs, the City fathers continued with their policy of demolition of the central slums (which were in fact often distinguished Georgian areas), and building new outer suburban housing so that the trend towards depopulation in the centre increased. This left a huge acreage inhabited by a handful of caretakers. Many of the houses to be sacrificed were tenanted and in poor repair and probably the majority of residents were glad to move even to the raw open spaces of Hartcliffe. But owner occupiers who wanted to stay were poorly treated and offered pitiful sums for their houses by the Corporation. Many empty spaces created by clearance, particularly in Bedminster and St. Philips, are still derelict twenty years later. The University and the Hospital Board had been allocated huge precincts on Kingsdown, north of the Centre, and sites were cleared, to remain ever since as car parks or derelict sites. But things did not go quite smoothly in one part of Kingsdown where the University and the Hospital Board had been allocated Comprehensive Redevelopment Areas on either side of St. Michael's Hill. In the end, the University did not use its compulsory powers and most of the street has now been saved, with the Hospital Board relinquishing its hold on some of the land at the

Repetitive 'Lego' of the speculative office development: the emergence of the faceless city.

lower end. Interestingly, where the University did demolish two houses on the frontage there is still an ugly gap site.

When the two big issues of the redevelopment of Wine Street and the City Docks arose, ordinary people came in large numbers to the Public Meetings. Those individuals and groups who had been fighting for a decade and who were in despair about what was proposed for the City saw that they were not alone; hundreds and probably thousands of other people felt the same way about the new buildings and the disappearing character and individuality of Bristol. The man in the street began to see that planning could no longer be left to councillors and professionals.

The Clifton and Hotwells Improvement Society, formed in 1968, was the first of the local amenity groups. CHIS set the pattern for the later ones. A small annual membership subscription was charged and an undertaking given to let members know of planning applications close to their homes. An essentially lay committee commented on anything it considered objectionable and encouraged individual members to do so as well. Over the next decade a further eight societies were formed in addition to action groups which arose to fight specific proposals. In the early days the comments of the amenity societies were often ignored by officers, without being relayed to the Planning Committee which continued to pass plans in spite of the poor quality of design and regardless of overall planning considerations.

CHIS was soon ranged alongside the older societies in fighting the City's plan for the Docks, and the planning proposals for the hotel in the Avon Gorge.

In 1971 after the Hotel Inquiry had demonstrated that success was possible, the Bristol Visual and Environmental Group was launched using the techniques developed previously of gaining wide publicity through press reports and leaflet distribution. Members of the public were encouraged to write either to the Secretary of State at the Department of the Environment or to the City Planning Officer. Leaflets were published detailing current threats, and the local press was extremely helpful in airing these matters. The group published leaflets on the Post Office Tower, the City Centre, the designation of Conservation Areas (only Henbury was designated in 1971), the Outer Circuit Road, over-supply of offices, the eyesore Hospital Precinct, housing policy, the City Docks, threats to Whiteladies Road, poor design of new buildings and the threats to innumerable historical buildings and areas like St. James Churchyard, Host Street and Brunswick Square. These leaflets bore fruit and individual issues began to hit the national press and were featured on television. Many plans were modified in the face of public reaction, but other matters had to be resolved at public inquiries, where societies acting together put, in nine cases out of ten, a winning case, often against large developers and local authorities. BVEG co-ordinated the amenity society case at many of them where a professional case against developers and sometimes local authorities was mounted.

Lack of money was not a great handicap. Most of the expert witnesses and other workers for amenity society cases gave their services freely because they cared for the character of Bristol. The sense of commitment and knowledge that they were able to bring to the issues often contrasted very strongly with the cold professionalism of the developer's case.

More recently, local authority representatives and amenity societies have been able to work together on the same side at many enquiries. It is, however, unfortunately true that although cases were won and developers thwarted, repair notices to protect buildings from decay and vandalism were not issued. Many groups of buildings owned by frustrated developers have been allowed to deteriorate almost beyond recall.

Only during the last two years when Historic Buildings Council money has been available has a start been made on refurbishing some of the buildings. Much larger sums of public money are often needed because repair notices were not issued at the right time. The houses at 78–100 St. Michael's Hill are a typical example. Originally the eleven buildings could have been restored for well under £100,000 to secure about forty flats; in 1979 restoration was costing £500,000. The lesson is really one for central as well as local government: a stitch in time is far cheaper than last-ditch rescue. . . . Local authorities have a duty to take enforcement action as soon as inquiry decisions are known, but very rarely is such action taken.

During the time of lay involvement there has been a gradual improvement in the design of new buildings. In the old days it often seemed that the planners would accept any old thing designed to make a maximum profit for a minimum outlay. Lay agitation has helped to promote a different attitude; amenity societies no longer want merely inoffensive or replica buildings. They want something exciting, which takes into account its context. They believe that all new development in the City should make a positive contribution to the quality of the environment. This can often best be achieved by the most modern of designs that are sensitive in terms of proportion, scale and materials to the surroundings and the function.

Other local societies have been set up: at Henbury, Westbury, Redland and Cotham, St. Paul's and Montpelier, Sneyd Park, Bishopston, Henleaze, Stapleton, Kingsdown and Kingsweston. These are all on the Clifton and Hotwells model. Action groups in Totterdown and St. George have grown up rather differently.

Height of folly

My delight in reading your report of the improvements to the Theatre Royal, is, I'm afraid, completely marred when I remember that the outside appearance is to be destroyed.

I refer of course to the G.P.O.'s grotesque proposal for a 305 foot high slab block to be built immediately behind the theatre. The figures are bad enough but I did not realise the full enormity of this plot until I made a scale drawing.

It then became vividly clear why the Fine Arts Commission condemn this tower in their 21st report and why it is being so strongly opposed by Mr. Arthur Palmer, M.P., and Ald. Jenkins.

I am sure that no Bristolian looking at this sketch, and with concern for the Theatre Royal, will be fobbed off by arguments that cables can't be extended and this monstrous box for machinery and cooking apparatus be built in a less obtrusive form and place.

I understand that our Planning Committee can now refuse permission and are only deterred by their undertakings when Circular 100 applied to the Post Office and by arguments about cost and convenience.

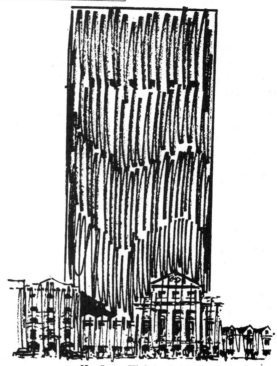

Mr. Jerry Hicks's sketch.

They should not be intimidated. It cost a lot to remove sewage from city centres, to build a railway under London and to defend our cities from wartime destruction. If we are resolute in our demands for a human environment the means to provide it and protect it can and will be found.

Jerry Hicks.
Goldrush, St. George Street, Bristol.

Letters to the press were a potent means of arousing public awareness.

From the 1970s: a satirical view of the future for Bristol.

Several societies have undertaken restoration work and other community projects. At Westbury, the village hall has been refurbished, at Hotwells, Hope Chapel has been converted into a community centre. At Bedminster, the City Farm was established on waste ground. Groups of individuals have restored buildings, as in Hope Square and St. Michael's Hill, with conservationist aims largely in line with those of the societies.

Local amenity societies are linked with those in other parts of the County of Avon through Avon Amenity Societies Liaison Organisation. Realising that what is happening in the 'rural' areas affects what happens in the city and vice versa, the City societies have become concerned about the establishment of dormitory towns which generate commuter traffic; issues such as the siting of hypermarkets, industrial estates and power stations, Severn Barrage, Avon Metro, airports and so on, all affect both town and country.

A major issue, very much alive at present, is the pressure to develop suburban green field sites, playing fields, golf courses and hospital parkland, usually for housing. This may be particularly ill-advised when there is so much derelict land in the City Centre. Currently the amenity societies are concerned about the spread of large scale offices and shopping centres into residential suburbs, where developers are attracted because of the streets available for car parking, careless of the degradation this will bring to attractive environments. The spread of clubs, licensed for drinking and gambling, is a particular menace on the fringes of the central area while the proliferation of building society offices, boutiques and antique shops in what used to be good neighbourhood shopping areas providing food and services seems irresistible, however sympathetic the City Council may be to the basic needs of the community.

In 1977, following a request from the Bristol Amenity Societies, a Conservation Panel was set up. The standing members are the city-wide societies and local society representatives who are asked to comment on applications in their area. The panel is predominantly of laymen, apart from a representative from the Bristol Society of Architects; a sensible composition which was decided by the Planning Committee. The panel ensures that critical listed building and conservation issues do not go by default, provided local authority officers have identified them.

The involvement of the ordinary lay public in planning decisions, and the willingness of the City Council to listen, has been greatly helped by the local press, particularly the *Bristol Evening Post*. Another critical factor was the appointment of a new city planning officer in 1975. Mr. Jim Preston's dedication to urban design and his recruitment to the Planning Department of able and sensitive officers was of paramount importance.

The revision of Bristol's list of Buildings of Architectural and Historic Interest, originally made in the 1940s, added 1,500 buildings to the Statutory List. This meant that new plans had to be made for many groups of buildings previously run-down for redevelopment, particularly groups of small shops immediately round the central business area. The collapse of demand for large scale offices took place around 1974 and it has taken some time to secure the piecemeal rehabilitation of buildings which would have been demolished if they had not been listed. Rehabilitation is now well under way, providing a variety of small shops, small service industries – the ideal infrastructure for starting up independent small businesses, now recognised as an important factor in the economic life of the country.

The situation has not much changed with regard to transport planning. Most city councillors responsible for the massive road and office development policies of the previous decade and for the plans to fill in the harbour, went to the new Avon County Council which was formed in 1974. With them went a large number of highway engineers who had formulated the £400 million worth of road schemes identified on the development plan map. Fortunately, lack of money has forced them to abandon a great many road proposals – or they would still be causing untold blight in the City – but there is still cause for grave disquiet. Whereas any householder must apply for planning permission for a small extension to his home – and rightly, because something ugly and inappropriate can have a distressing effect on his neighbours and the character of the street – huge road schemes, costing millions of pounds and causing untold dereliction and degradation to whole neighbourhoods, can be added to the annual Transport Programme submission(TPP) without any public comment or consultation. Planning permission is only sought years later, when blight has done its work.

The Chairman of Avon County Council, as Chairman of the County Councils Association, made the astonishing complaint to the Minister that there is too much public participation in transport planning, when apart from the new Public Transport consultation there is simply no opportunity for the public to comment at all. The improvement seen in the built environment when attention is paid to public comment, suggests transport plans should also be subject to comment at a very early stage in their formulation.

What is especially valuable about amenity societies is the forum they provide for lay people with a special interest in urban design, historic buildings and planning. Such groups can make a vital contribution to democracy. Party attitudes and vested interest groups within councils sometimes prevent proper debate in council committees, and matters therefore have to be raised outside so that they are properly aired and policies re-examined. Much of the onus of this falls on the local press, but the press itself needs special interest groups to raise the issues and stimulate debate.

From the societies' point of view, it is obviously much easier to keep groups together when there are battles to fight than when there is only the large amount of routine checking, research and comment necessary if they are to make a useful contribution to the planning process. From this point of view, it is much healthier if there is a continual stream of new societies to augment and stimulate the older-established, and no-one should ever be deterred from setting up a new group by the existence of older ones. The recently formed 'Cyclebag' is a particularly welcome addition of the last two years. In a city like Bristol there will always be too much for established societies to do and too few willing hands.

PART II

PLANNING AND PROTEST: Case studies
Introduction

The idea of planners and community in opposition seems a contradiction in terms. The planners' job is to serve society by operating a control system that allows development which provides advantage to the community as a whole. The ideal project is one that allows a land owner or developer to achieve what he desires in terms of economics and function whilst making an improvement to the environment of the area in which he is developing for the ordinary citizen as well as the specialist user. In 1980 the planners' phrase 'planning gain' summarises this. In 1960 it was less clearly understood; planning gain was a somewhat abstract vision incorporated in a development plan or in a paper dream of 'comprehensive development'. The plans had been published, the public consulted, it was then the planners' job to work towards the published ends.

Vision and reality proved to be widely divergent. The planners had an immensely difficult job to tackle. Developers were either hard-headed businessmen or determined politicians; money and time were short; the paper plans were either not explicit enough or too ideal. Almost invariably the buildings, as they emerged from the process, were more nearly what the developers wanted than what the community had been anticipating.

Protest from the amenity societies was usually a reaction not against 'change' in itself but against change for the worse. This phase in Bristol covered the main part of the City's post war development right up to the end of the 1960s and into the 1970s.

In the post war years and right into the 1970s, property developers made money all over the country; in London, Office Development Permits had to be introduced to slow the rate at which the old city was disappearing before the march of the office blocks. These did not apply to Bristol. Anyone could see the commercial attractions of a city which was to be at the junction of the M4 and M5, and offered a marvellous range of recreational and cultural facilities for workers. Offices sprang up like weeds, mainly built 'on spec' for letting. For the most part their design was of the lowest standard acceptable to the planners. The procedure was for planners to agree with the developer a floor space index which governed the area of accommodation allowable on a given site, and the overall size of the building. Thereafter it was all up to the architect and his client, the speculative developer.

Building generally consisted of boxes, flat or tall as appropriate and arranged so as to cram as many standard sized and shaped units on the site as the planners would allow. There were of course exceptions. In the main these were the buildings erected for occupation by their owners, where an attractive or impressive appearance was part of the building's function: the Robinson Building, the Bristol United Press headquarters and the Phoenix Assurance offices. Even these, well designed in themselves, tended to lack respect or feel for their surroundings.

By the early seventies road and office building had reached their peak. The City Centre was a mass of hoardings. Sometimes these concealed building sites; more often vacant lots. Land was snapped up whenever it came on the market and often before. Until the passing of the Civic Amenities Act in 1967, there was in practice no control over the demolition of historic buildings in Bristol. Whatever lawyers might say, the planning authority took the view that demolition even of listed buildings did not require planning permission. Even after the passing of the Act, the planners were easily persuaded that buildings were not capable of restoration at reasonable cost. Indeed, in several cases they supported demolition which indirectly assisted their long-term road plans. The City Corporation owned several historic buildings which were demolished or allowed to decay, or negotiated with developers who intended to demolish them.

This is the context in which the amenity societies fought their most difficult battles in Bristol.

'Package deal' blocks of flats of the type intended for High Kingsdown: their bleakness and unimaginative landscaping contrasted with the rich textures and landscaping of the scheme which finally won the day.

What happened in Kingsdown

Kingsdown was Bristol's most important early Georgian suburb. It rose in terraces on the steep slopes to the north west of the Centre, a mixture of well built, elegant houses for professional classes, interspersed with cottages for the less affluent, linked by steep steps and cobbled alleys. It was described in the *BSA Journal* of 1952, when, though war-damaged, it was virtually intact. Most of the buildings were of brick; the area had a rather sombre quality and lacked the popular appeal of the leafier suburbs.

The smallest of the five areas that make up Kingsdown lies to the south of St. Michael's Hill, in the University Precinct, and includes Tankard's Close. This was the most worn out and least defended area. By the time the vast University Engineering Building began, it had suffered twenty years of what is now called planning blight. Fortunately, largely due to the opposition of the Rector of St. Michael's Church, who was rapidly losing all his parishioners, the south side of St. Michael's Hill was not demolished.

The main development on the hillsides in the second area took place in the mid-sixties by which time feeling in favour of conservation had begun to grow. Resistance from local people, the intervention of the Royal Fine Arts Commission, and – unexpectedly for 1963/64 – an alternative, low level architectural proposal for the site, were of no avail. The eighteenth century planned grid iron, with horizontal contour and stepped vertical streets, laid out like a Greek Colonial city, was wiped out, and the great fourteen-storey slabs went up at the rear of King Square.

The resistance groups were learning the ropes, however, and when the time came for the third area of clearance – on the plateau between St. Michael's Hill and Alfred Place – they were quicker off the mark. This area had become one of almost total dereliction and was a great embarrassment to the Labour administration who were in any case worried about their record in house-building. In the late 1960s, with an election looming, they

45

instituted what was to prove a visually and probably socially disastrous series of proposals for 'package deal' blocks of flats, of the sort which had begun to appear all over the Bristol skyline. An emergency scheme to build three of these blocks on the Kingsdown II site was cobbled up in 1968. Because no system then operated in the Civic Society for regularly inspecting the planning register the project was not spotted until it was almost too late. The contract had been negotiated and, in December, the Planning Committee was about to award itself planning permission to allow the Housing Committee to proceed to build the towers on this most prominent hill top.

However, at the last moment, a lawyer resident of Kingsdown informed and activated all those who might help to frustrate this latest and most insensitive desecration of the Georgian suburb. The planners and various officials had to be threatened before details of the proposals could be obtained. The amenity societies, residents, conservationists, newspaper men, Opposition councillors and the Royal Fine Arts Commission were all called into action but nothing it seemed could stop the council from completing the due processes that had been set in motion. It was only hours before the crucial council meeting that a telephone call from the Secretary of the Royal Fine Arts Commission persuaded them not to proceed with the scheme. A great victory had been achieved.

The council set in motion a new development plan for the site, by appointing a private firm of architects as consultants to devise a low level, medium-density housing scheme. A few months later, the new Conservative Council chose to sell the site but, fully aware of the background, they required those who tendered for the site to carry out a development on the lines of the consultants' plan. The result, 'High Kingsdown', is one of the few respectable new projects to emerge from the agonising history of Kingsdown in the 1950s and 1960s, and indeed it has won several awards and brought great credit to the City.

Between St. Michael's Hill and Marlborough Hill a huge site of over eighteen acres had been designated as the Precinct for the District Hospital. Then a new BRI block was built facing Upper Maudlin Street: next, the Radio Physics block: finally,

Kingsdown: local authority housing. The 18th century gridiron, laid out like a Greek Colonial City on its steep hillside was wiped out and these 14 storey slabs went up in its place.

and visually most offensively, the Maternity Hospital, brutalism at its most crude, took its place on the St. Michael's Hill frontage. These buildings completely ignored their context: existing buildings, and the shape and contours of the site. They are surrounded by waste space and car parks. £4¼ million was spent on the Maternity Hospital and the interest charges alone equalled more than half the total cost of running the older maternity hospitals.

In the streets around the new hospital buildings, more and more Georgian and Victorian houses were acquired by the Hospital Board. The occupants, many of them elderly, were paid derisory sums and forced to leave the area. In Gloucester Place the owners of the twelve small cottages were offered a maximum of £100 for their homes. Buddleia grew on the site for fifteen years until an amenity society cleared it up. There are still no plans for the site, but the Hospital refuse to sell it.

47

Two faces of Kingsdown. Hospital buildings surrounded by waste space and car parks; Alfred Place, typical modest Georgian houses now being restored.

What Happened in Kingsdown

The first victory for conservationists against the Hospital Board came in 1972, when it was proposed to demolish numbers 78–100 St. Michael's Hill and replace them with brick flats for medical accommodation. Amenity society members and students re-painted one of the houses to show how the buildings would look if rehabilitated. 'Save the Terrace' proclaimed a sign, rapidly expunged by the Hospital authorities who, while inordinately slow about any rehabilitation, acted with alacrity when they felt their plans to be threatened. The City Council, as a result of petitions and letters from medical students and conservationists, placed a Preservation Order on the Georgian buildings, but the Hospital Board made no attenpt to reconsider their policy. Architectural students were turned over to the police when they measured the buildings to cost rehabilitation. Hospital workmen took lead off some of the buildings. It is only now that a hospital charity has at last restored the houses. The work was carried out with the help of a grant from the Historic Buildings Council – and beautifully done, but at a cost of five times the original estimate from the Hospital Board's own consultants in 1972.

Meantime, the Board was demolishing houses as soon as they were acquired and the vast area of dereliction continued to grow. Thirteen good houses in Halsbury Road were largely destroyed by Hospital employees so that they could not be occupied by students. When the Kingsdown Conservation Group was formed, it increased pressure on the Department of the Environment to list the Georgian buildings in the Precinct which had not been demolished. The Hospital Board was warned and began to demolish those which it owned, but the Department of the Environment at last spot listed what was left. This saved the bottom of St. Michael's Hill from demolition and road widening, and parts of Kingsdown Parade and Marlborough Hill. Residents and interested parties were now urged to write to the Secretary of State for Health and Social Services about the appalling blight and dereliction caused by the Hospital Board, and urging a reduction in the Precinct, the release and sale of existing Georgian houses within it, clearing and landscaping the derelict car parks and a coherent plan for any further development on the Precinct. The Hospital Board was forced to rethink its ambitious plans. Five years later a good deal of landscaping and restoration has been done, the Health Authority has made good use of the Job Creation Scheme. However, it continues to hold acres of land covered only with car parks. It has refused private offers for Georgian houses in areas which, because of the gradients, it can never develop for hospital purposes. There is still no coherent plan for further development, and in any case, only one more ward block is likely to be built. More public accountability for hospital administrators is urgently needed.

In spite of all the destruction, Kingsdown on the hilltop – Alfred Place, Kingsdown Parade and Somerset Street – survived. It was restored by private individuals as family homes which now sell for good prices. Gradually the derelict gap sites are being filled by housing associations, which have produced some delightful designs. St. Michael's Hill has two gap sites still – one left derelict by the University for years. The Maternity Hospital, however concealed by trees, will always be a brutal affront to the street, but the rest is emerging again as one of the loveliest streets in Bristol.

Some of the remaining infill developments in Kingsdown are already planned and seem to be likely to make a good contribution to the rehabilitation of an area that has suffered from much vandalism of a type not imposed by teenagers, but care is still needed. At the time of writing good, eighteenth century brick-work here is being plastered over thoughtlessly. Our heritage of examples of past building skills is still diminishing. All that remains must be protected zealously.

Bristol City Docks

Few could have guessed that the announcement, in the *Bristol Civic News* of August 1969, that the Council was to promote a Parliamentary Bill enabling the City to withdraw navigation rights in a declining dock would provoke a hitherto acquiescent public and, ultimately, produce landmarks in alternative planning. Had the architects of the Bill sought only to restrict the historical navigation rights of commercial shipping its passage might have been untroubled by most of the amenity societies. But the planners saw an opportunity to fill in large sections of the Floating Harbour to create more land for commercial development and for roads.

The proposed in-fill was euphemistically described in the *Civic News* as the substitution of 'a lagoon system'; but despite the document's modest circulation the danger was quickly apparent. The threatened removal of tall masts from the harbour was a prospect which disturbed the average Bristolian even more than the proliferation of tower blocks. The idea of destroying the City Docks struck at the very heart of the historical port which above all gave the City its individual flavour. Certainly the word spread rapidly and events followed in rapid succession. First, a public meeting was called at the Folk House by four separate amenity groups: Bristol Civic Society, Clifton and Hotwells Improvement Society, Cabot Cruising Club and the Inland Waterways Association. Speakers included Paul Chadd, barrister, who volunteered his professional services which were to prove critical, and Lord Methuen whose subsequent speech in the House of Lords helped to secure vital amendments. Next – at a packed and stormy meeting arranged by the City in the Colston Hall – the protestors politely took over the platform and overwhelmingly carried the motion to abandon the Bill. Then the City Council organised a Town Poll. They obtained support, with one exception, from the entire Council. The City's public relations men then helped persuade the public that amenity use of the Docks depended on the

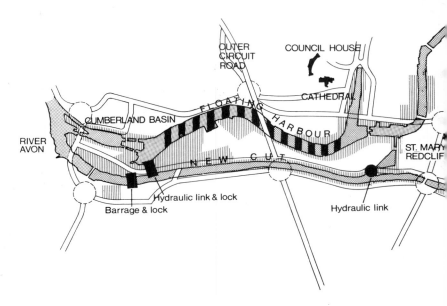

From the news sheet produced by the City Council: the original proposals for the City Docks. 'Partially reclaimed' meant 'filled in'.

Bill's enactment and a majority vote was secured. This decisive argument has since proved fallacious.

Through the efforts of Paul Chadd, Arthur Palmer, MP, and others, vital amendments were obtained in both Houses of Parliament to prevent any reduction in the water surface and to preserve navigation rights for small craft. During this period Charles Hill's shipyard withdrew their opposition which eased the passage of the Bill; the generous compensation terms granted to the company were not published until 1976. As the amended Bill would not take effect until 1980 the protestors now called for a Master Planner to study the Docks, and the City responded as they had done when faced with hostility over their Wine Street policy. They appointed Casson, Conder and Partners as consultants.

In describing the architectural spirit of the age in a television

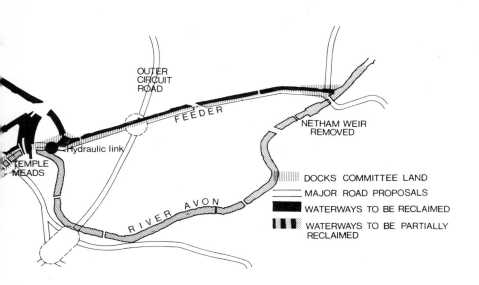

OUTER CIRCUIT ROAD

FEEDER

NETHAM WEIR REMOVED

Hydraulic link

TEMPLE MEADS

RIVER AVON

▨ DOCKS COMMITTEE LAND

── MAJOR ROAD PROPOSALS

▬ WATERWAYS TO BE RECLAIMED

▮▮▮ WATERWAYS TO BE PARTIALLY RECLAIMED

series, Sir Hugh said, 'What has happened, quite simply, and within two generations, is the beginning of a customers' revolt – a refusal any longer to be totally the vicitims of experts, a growing insistence on having more say in the shape of our surroundings'. He may well have been drawing on his experience in Bristol.

The official brief from the City required him to include three low fixed bridges over the harbour for motorways which would consume most of the adjacent land, the remainder of which was expected to contain a substantial amount of office building. However an *ad hoc* group of environmentalists informally appealed to Sir Hugh to design for people (and tall ships) which could restore life in the City Centre.

The 1972 Redevelopment Study produced by Casson attempted to resolve these conflicting demands and included an outspoken criticism of the City's road schemes which were seen in full for the first time: 'the proposals for the Outer Circuit Road crossing the Floating Harbour and the multi-level junction on the south bank should most seriously be re-considered. An area which in any event will require a substantial distribution road network cannot accommodate an urban motorway of this scale without very great disturbance to its unique character and a loss of the opportunity for making this area fit for pedestrian enjoyment. . . . Finally, however, a strict control over car usage in the area is essential and this will inevitably mean a reduction in the number of car parking spaces to be provided in office developments and the introduction of a public transport system geared to the users' requirements.' These comments reinforced the current 'Campaign to Stop the Outer Circuit Road' (whose organisers not only forecast a threat to the Docks but had commissioned engineers to produce an alternative scheme). However, the urban motorway concept which the architects were compelled to accept as part of their brief unbalanced the remainder of the report. Following a public discussion at the Corn Exchange, organised by the *Evening Post*, when it was realised that no fairy godfather was going to achieve a solution, the Bristol City Docks Group was formed and began the process that was to transform organised protest into alternative planning.

In 1971 the RIBA conference in Bristol was told of a surrealist underground organisation called DODO which was engaged in a grotesque plot to transform Bristol into Birmingham – an essential part of which was to fill in the Docks and the Gorge. Since this satirical ridicule was a surprisingly consistent explanation of so much post war planning, DODO lectures were called for in a wide variety of alarmed circles, and DODO's activities were reported in *The Times*.

More seriously, a steady flow of written protest poured into the local press and the Department of the Environment. Bristol became national news and support came from beyond the City.

A change in direction began in 1973 when the Bristol City Docks Group produced the first of a series of reports. Starting from an empirical standpoint the Group asked questions about the quality of the City environment and its essential ingredients. When the general principles which emerged were applied to the City Docks it was agreed that the critical needs were:

A diversity of major functions. Those could include land and

The Docks back in use : power boat racing now a popular annual event.

water-based light industry and recreation, museums, shops and above all a large residential content to offset the drift from the City Centre. This concept of diversity was dramatically opposed to the zoning maps which dominated planning offices.

Low rise, high density living accommodation. Casson generally accepted the case for low rise housing but his densities were too low to support a rich diversity of associated amenities. The Group demonstrated the possibility of increasing the residential content of the Docks.

A mixture of well-integrated old and new buildings. The consequent need for sensitive restoration and conversion of buildings not protected by 'listing' procedures was agreed by Casson for aesthetic reasons, and the success of St. Katharine's Dock in London helped to convince Bristol of the commercial viability of conversion.

Reduction of the impact of motor cars. The urgent need for traffic control, improved alternative transport including bus, train, cycle, boat and adequate footpaths is now increasingly appreciated by Bristol City planners, though Avon, the highway authority, still has a major preoccupation with motor cars. The success of pedestrian precincts in many places has begun to attract commuters back to live in the city centres.

Maximum exploitation of the water. The recreational value of the Floating Harbour 'with the s.s. *Great Britain* as a magnificent centre piece' was fully appreciated by Casson although greatly constrained by the road plans. However, perhaps the need to keep open the options for transporting heavy goods by water is becoming more and more apparent in spite of North Sea Oil.

The BCDG reports set out these principles and suggested the form which such proposals might take. Sketches and photo-montages were produced to suggest guidelines and to introduce the public and planners to the exciting possibilities which lay ahead. The impact of these publications must be seen in the light

s.s. Great Britain: *a magnificent focal point.*

of a complex series of events and influences. Perhaps the most important of these were the return of the s.s. *Great Britain* in 1970 and the series of Water Festivals and power boat races which have focussed public attention on the amenity value of the harbour. The commercial use of the Docks had precluded public use and it came as a pleasant surprise to Bristolians to see their potential even slightly realised. The original reluctance of the City to provide permanent mooring for the *Great Britain* probably had something to do with its presence on the line of the Outer Circuit Road, but the return of the rusty old hulk up the Avon produced an extraordinary public reaction. Cheering crowds strewed it with rose petals from Brunel's Suspension Bridge and later poured through the turnstiles in their thousands to be reminded of Bristol's past maritime pre-eminence. Nor was this exclusively local pride; visitors from far and wide included Prince Philip whose outspoken support for the restoration in its original dock did much to persuade the reluctant hosts that the old girl was here to stay. The

Arnolfini out-of-doors.

civic approval she is now accorded is one of many signs of a new sympathy.

The Arnolfini, which moved to 'W' Shed before converting Bush Warehouse, demonstrated the potential in the Docks for cultural purposes and the value of old buildings in that setting.

The *Bristol Evening Post* played a critical part in public education during this period. Not only did it provide a general forum for comment over five years but at regular intervals presented major articles on the Docks' future. A key feature on Bristol Docks, the well-timed appraisal of St. Katharine's Dock and a great number of constructive editorials are examples of a sustained campaign to inform and educate. Television also gave occasional publicity to the Docks debate and the short-lived *Bristol Channel* helped the BCDG make their own film.

An example of growing co-operation between planners and environmentalists in promoting creative thought was the organisation of two exhibitions in the City Art Gallery under the title of *Twenty ideas for Bristol*. In these, a large number of suggestions for the Docks were presented.

The upsurge in interest and positive public support for the Docks as a new feature of Bristol's community life, coupled with financial stringencies, finally created a climate which was to promote the abandonment of the Docks Bill. Bristol and Avon set up a joint Study Team which in 1977 produced *The Opportunities for the Docks*, a forerunner of The Local Plan, which enshrines many of the ideas which the Docks Group promoted.

The *Great Britain* and Arnolfini are both supported by public and private funds. The Bristol Water Festival was launched by boat clubs but is now sponsored by the City which has also encouraged a Wine Festival and a Boat Show. Narrow-boat trips are a private inspiration and a non-profit making company has paid for the retention of cranes and the reintroduction of a ferry service. The City and Bristol Civic Society have jointly promoted and financed tree planting. Two floating pubs have been launched with official encouragement. Water recreation is developing through the joint efforts of the City and a voluntary Bristol Sports Association. Artists rent space in a warehouse and the Bristol Arts Centre has negotiated a lease of parts of 'W' Shed and the attractive 'E'

The Edwardian baroque facade of 'E' Shed, and the warehouse behind it, splendidly restored by the City under its conservation programme.

Shed (which is immediately adjacent to the City Centre), for an ambitious cultural and social centre.

This combination of voluntary effort encouraged by Bristol City is visibly transforming what might once have seemed a depressing area in which to build houses into what should now be an attractive proposition for both developers and potential residents. If one compares this image with the 'DODO' tower blocks and prairie housing estates of the 1950s and 1960s one understands what Casson means by a 'consumer revolt'.

The Docks are now beginning to play a vital role in the City's life again – and not merely as an extension of the City's entertainment and cultural life. One housing development is being built; albeit architecturally disappointing, it will be the first major injection of residential accommodation here, to be followed by others. The sand boats still come into the harbour every day. Every effort should be made to encourage this industrial use to continue here. There may be a marginal nuisance with this, but the advantages of keeping it far outweigh any disadvantages. Bristol Docks must develop not as a paper-thin tourist site but as a real place, where people live and work and others come to enjoy the incomparable qualities of the watersides, with their fine buildings and constant activity.

The Bristol City Docks saga suggests that this is not a politically inspired revolt with a hierarchical centre, though a small but increasing number of politicians have been involved, nor is it an hysterical banner-waving demonstration of anarchy. It is, on the contrary, the spontaneous formation of informal network organisations with multiple moving centres by concerned and caring people. The fight against the Bristol City Docks Bill provided the catalyst.

The grass roots response has been so well described by Sir Hugh Casson that he should have the last word:

'The qualities we are beginning to look for in our architecture are not so often the elegant gestures of strong statements, glad as we are for their occasional appearance, but modesty and common sense, suitability and reassurance, a sense of shared decisions and of the importance of the individual, and a respect for what is already there. The spirit of this new age, in my view, is the rediscovery of the truth – often obscured beneath the stylistic nit-picking of the experts and historians – that architecture is not just buildings, it is places . . . buildings and spaces and landscapes and light and weather and movement and people, all warmed by a concern for human life. This is architecture – "work done", as Lethaby said, "by human beings for human beings", and thus truly expressive of our times.'

The Grand Spa Hotel

News of the proposal to build an extension to the Grand Spa Hotel (now known as the Avon Gorge Hotel) on land below Princes Lane broke in January 1971, two years after the publication of the Skeffington Report on public participation in planning and one year after the Civic Amenities Act which first enshrined ·its recommendations. No building proposal before or since has created such public furore in Bristol, possibly in Britain, in terms of the scale of media interest. It must be compared with the proposals for Piccadilly Circus of the 1950s, and some of the classic battles of the 1960s over the siting of supergrid electricity routes.

The site was beside Brunel's Suspension Bridge in an area that could be described as having been 'left over' after the eighteenth and nineteenth century development of Clifton. It was perhaps in a slightly ambiguous condition in planning development terms, in spite of its location at the head of the stunningly beautiful Gorge and under Clifton's celebrated Suspension Bridge. The Corporation and the developer had to move swiftly in order to meet a timetable that had been imposed from outside. The Planning Committee and its officers were not committed in any way to the idea of consultation with outside agencies on planning matters; indeed they were distinctly hostile to what they saw as interference in a planning process which was primarily a matter of encouraging development through negotiation between civic authority and developer.

A reconstruction of the timetable is difficult because there is little information available about the preliminaries to the planning application which was registered on January 6th 1971. At the Public Inquiry in May of that year, the then City Planning Officer, the late James Bennett, stated that in 'late 1969' a proposal was submitted for a 'multistorey car park with a block of flats on top'. He also described the genesis of the project and demonstrated how planners and developers worked together. It seems that the developers originally entered into informal discussions with the planning authority about the conversion of the Grand Spa's out-dated ballroom into a discotheque. The planners' response was to recommend the investigation of off street parking for the hotel. They were aware that local residents were upset by noise, congestion and nuisance created by the weekly public dances. The developers submitted an outline plan for a car park. Someone, perhaps a planner, suggested that flats on top of the car park would make good economic sense and would allow a more 'architectural' solution.

Presumably it was only in the last months of 1970 that the developers spotted the existence of the Promotion of Tourism Act which allowed the English Tourist Board to promote the building of new hotel accommodation by giving grants of up to £1,000 per bedroom to hoteliers. It must have been a busy time for the designers. By January, the scheme, now a hotel extension atop a car park, was complete. It was to house 203 cars, banqueting facilities for 250 people, 126 double rooms and a dozen or so single ones. The proposed building was eight storeys and 30 m high, 80 m long and 180 m from the Clifton tower of the Suspension Bridge. All this apparently had grown out of a project to up-date a dance hall. The concept had emerged in the course of discussions between planners and developers. This was normal of course; other hotels were built here, with support from Tourist Board funds, but in this case, the need to act swiftly, and a complete failure on the planners' part to see all the implications of their decisions, was not normal.

The Promotion of Tourism Act and the possibility of a £126,000 grant – worth £¼ million in 1980 values – was about to run out. The last date at which developers could claim was in March 1971 and to qualify for grant a 'substantial start' had to be made by then. At that time the average time taken to process planning applications was six months. There were just twenty-two days between the registration of the application and the Planning Committee's award of outline permission.

The young Clifton and Hotwells Improvement Society were responsible for discovering the application and for starting the reaction against it. A meeting of interested people was called and an *ad hoc* action committee called 'STAG' (Save the Avon Gorge)

How the protesters saw the proposed hotel in the Avon Gorge.

set up as soon as the scale of the project was realised. By January 27th 1971, the day of the Planning Committee meeting, the Corporation had received 174 letters objecting to the proposal. The Planning Committee was not at full strength for this meeting and some members present abstained on a vote but the Planning Officer's recommendation to grant outline approval was agreed. Two members voted against. The local newspapers were publishing letters and were beginning to take a stance on the issue. The Royal Fine Arts Commission had already given a qualified approval to the design which no doubt persuaded councillors that they were right to act precipitately in the face of already vociferous objection.

In 1971 both the Labour and Conservative parties in Bristol stood firmly and defensively against the amenity societies whose informed criticisms of the City's post war planning and architecture record seemed damaging to political reputations. The objectors at that stage were not fully organised but to the councillors they were the 'same old lot'. In fact, they were not. Bristol's planning reputation was widely known outside the City. Within days, STAG was acting as a clearing house for objections flowing in from all over the country. The lawyers advised that Planning Committee decisions were legally binding and that only the Minister in Whitehall could interfere with the 'due processes' by instituting an Inquiry but that such interference was in any case rare and unlikely. STAG recognised the need to redirect pressure from Bristol to London and encouraged objectors to write to the Secretary of State for the Environment. As it happened, there was a postal strike. This potentially disastrous snag was turned to advantage with great ease. STAG organised its own delivery service, sending couriers to the Department of the Environment every second day with any letters delivered at a number of addresses around the town. The challenge clearly attracted people and letters flowed in. The couriers were soon delivering two hundred or more letters every other day. Correspondence appeared in *The Times*, *Guardian* and *Observer*, and out-of-Bristol objectors were advised that regional offices of the Department of the Environment were bound to send on letters addressed to the Minister in London. Eventually some 1,200 letters landed on the Minister's desk.

STAG was also preparing the ground for the hoped-for Inquiry. Solicitor members of the various amenity societies were at work and counsel was briefed. Local M.P.s joined in, Arthur Palmer and Robert Cooke being particularly active in lobbying and asking questions.

The flow of letters and rumblings from the establishment had their effect. Peter Walker, Environment Secretary, took action, called in the outline application and announced a public inquiry. This was on March 4th. Incredibly, after the Minister had announced his intention, rumours began to circulate that detailed drawings were to be submitted and that the Planning Committee would consider them. The possibility of compensation to the developer was being publicly discussed at that time, with suggestions that the City Council would be responsible and that compensation could amount to hundreds of thousands of pounds. It was perhaps this possibility that drove the councillors onwards. STAG publicised the rumour that the City Council's Planning Committee would indeed grant full planning permission on March 17th, 1971, and it also warned London in time for the Minister to make a second and absolutely unprecedented intervention. Only a few hours before the Planning Committee meeting the new drawings were called in via a telephone instruction to the Town Clerk from London. The intervention provides an illustration of the remarkably strong, direct level of contact that the *ad hoc* committee had achieved with Ministry officials in its few weeks of existence.

It could well be that the outcome of the Inquiry was determined on that day. It is one thing for a local authority to stand out against Whitehall with the local community behind it, but entirely another when the authority appears to be running in the face of powerful local opinion.

The bizarre nature of the 'Gorge Affair' was heightened in the following week, this time by the developers and their architects. Bulldozers appeared on site after the Minister's second intervention and concrete foundations were begun. Whether these were in the correct position has not been determined but they were meant to demonstrate the 'substantial start' to building works that would allow the developers to claim the Tourist grant. This move was

66

clearly unlawful although the local authority took no enforcement action. Works were discontinued after a few days of somewhat confused activity.

The Minister announced a first date for May 7th, 1971 which he was later persuaded to put back until 17th of that month.

April and the first half of May were spent by STAG in preparing its case. The strategy was to emphasise the impact of the proposed building on the Gorge visually and physically and to highlight the impact of the building's *function* on the surrounding neighbourhood. It was decided not to make much comment about the proposed architectural character of the building.

The Inquiry lasted nine days. The legal and expert witnesses called by the objectors gave their services freely or on minimum expenses. Although STAG controlled and mounted the objectors' case, other organisations were involved as well as many individuals and groups. The National Trust, the Georgian Group and the neighbouring local authority (which had not been consulted by Bristol) all took their part in supporting the objections.

The well-orchestrated case was put by experts, who included Sir John Betjeman and Sir James Richards (then J. M. Richards, editor of the *Architectural Review*). These two were unequivocal in their opinion which can be paraphrased by combining a statement from each into a composite: 'it is incredible that such vandalism could be contemplated to one of the most beautiful views in Europe'.

Professional planners, a geologist, architects, a traffic engineer and botanists were called to build up the case on the two main lines of attack of the unacceptable obtrusiveness of the building in the Gorge and its impact upon the surrounding environment.

The quality of the argument, the intellectual grasp shown by the objectors' lawyers, the brilliance with which Mr Paul Chadd Q.C. presented the case and the committed attitude of all who appeared for the objectors was exemplary and no doubt affected the Minister's Inspector, Mr. S. W. Midwinter, when he drew up his report, which was to recommend that the building proposed should not be approved.

The Outer Circuit Road

Membership of amenity groups tends to be drawn from the privileged and articulate sections of society. The plan for the outer circuit road in Bristol contained an area to the west and north, where topographical difficulties coincided with districts whose residents could be expected to cause the planners trouble. Proposals for great bridges, tunnels and cuttings across the Docks, the Clifton hillside and Whiteladies Road were not therefore taken altogether seriously although they had an immediate and disastrous effect upon property values; but the threat was vastly greater to the east and south of the City. In these areas, property was cheap, the topography was generally less difficult and the residents were thought to be less vociferous.

The road line went through residential areas considered to be in need of rebuilding and some were actually scheduled for this or were in fact being rebuilt as local authority developments at the critical time. The fact that the local Labour Party was in opposition for part of the time – and that most of the wards affected by the road plans were held by Labour – made little difference initially, for the plans had been introduced when they were in control.

The Civic Society had lost the first round of the battle by 1969 when the Development Plan Review containing the OCR was approved by the Minister. It had few contacts in the areas where the planners wished to start clearing and building, and there was a clear need for direct action amongst the population and their councillors.

In 1968 the St. Paul's Housing Group and a Bristol branch of Shelter were formed. In March, 1971, the St. Paul's Action Group was set up to fight the line of the road through St. Paul's and Montpelier. This was an offshoot of the Housing Group. At about this time, the Montpelier Residents Association also decided to try to get the line of the road changed. Both groups were concerned with the effect of the road on the housing and amenity of their areas and did not take any stance on the transport issues.

Between March and October, 1971, the Campaign against the

Outer Circuit Road began to establish itself as a political entity. Three people spent this period collecting facts on the history of the Development Plan, the reasons for the OCR, and planning procedures. Their aim was to prepare a sound case against the road plans and to investigate the level of support that could be found for the campaign. At the same time they looked for an alternative route that would be less damaging socially and environmentally. This they found readily. It had been proposed in the 1950s. The researchers made contacts with groups and individuals who could advise them and support the campaign. It was decided that the 'campaign' was not to be formally constituted but would remain a co-ordinating body and provide ideas, material and energy for anyone who opposed the road. By 1972 the public believed it to be an official organisation. It never was but it gained an important benefit by having that reputation. Until 1973, it avoided the internal dissent that can defeat pressure groups more effectively than external opposition. Contact was made with the *Evening Post* whose editor listened sympathetically and contact was also made with the planning correspondent of *The Times*.

An essential aim of the campaign was to inform everyone living on or near the line of the OCR and encourage them to write to the Secretary of State, Peter Walker (who had made bold speeches about urban environment in the 1971 election), the City Planning Officer, the councillors for the wards affected and of course the chairman and shadow chairman of the Planning Committee. This first period of intense, but essentially backstage, activity was followed by more public action. The first meetings with students to enlist their support and help with leafleting took place in October 1971. In November, the Campaign was launched with a major feature in the *Evening Post* which was followed by a supporting editorial. For the next six months hardly a day passed without a letter, article or report in that newspaper.

A leaflet campaign, spread over several months, concentrated on Cotham, Easton, Clifton, Totterdown and Southville.

The first public meeting took place in Easton, called by the local Residents Association. It was here that the City's plans were furthest advanced. Incredibly, the architects and housing officials and the committees involved had permitted a high density

The Outer Circuit Road churning its way through Easton.

housing project to be 'adjusted' to accommodate a six- and eight-lane highway through it. There was virtually no chance of stopping this stage I part of the OCR, and the Campaign, through its workers, made it clear to local residents that the chances were small. In 1972, public meetings were held in St. Paul's (organised by the Campaign), in Southville and Totterdown (organised by residents' groups). In the spring, the Campaign commissioned consultant engineers to report on the feasibility of an alternative route for traffic from Stage I going south. This alternative was published and formed the basis of subsequent arguments.

During that year, it was announced that a Land Use and Transportation Study would be set up for the whole of the Bristol region. The Campaign and Bristol Civic Society made contact with amenity societies in Bath and Saltford in order to mount joint pressure on the Secretary of State at the DOE to rule that the local authority should delay major road developments until the LUTS investigations had been completed and published.

The Campaign was much more directly involved with the

70

politicians and political party organisations than is usual for the amenity societies. Without this close contact there was little chance of success, for plans were well advanced and the politicians generally held strong views that linked the prestige of the City with the scale of its roadworks. At the beginning of the Campaign, political support for the OCR was solid. Few councillors were at all sympathetic to the Campaign. Even those in the Labour Party who were would not speak out in public, because of the bipartisan support for the OCR in the Council. The Campaign was, of course, a political pressure group. It had to find which of the two parties was more likely to change its official policy. Efforts were concentrated on increasing support for the Campaign among the ranks of local Labour councillors.

After intense pressure and activity within the Labour Party during 1972, the leadership was nearly defeated over the OCR and it became a matter of time before the policy changed substantially. Even so, it took too long and houses in Totterdown were destroyed without much opposition in the Council. Antagonism to the Campaign within the leadership of the Labour Party became fiercer towards the end of 1972 and the new Chairman of the Totterdown Residents Association, formed in part to attack the road, published a letter attacking the Campaign. This was the only occasion when there was public dissension and embarrass- ment.

As events turned out it had little effect. By mid-1973, the national policies on urban roads and housing had changed markedly. Redevelopment was becoming a dirty word; there was genuine concern about the environmental consequences of urban road schemes. Bristol played a small part in bringing about the change, but the bulk of the work was done elsewhere and earlier. The Campaign was able to draw on the experience of pressure groups in London and Manchester and of the City Council in Nottingham who were in the forefront of the battle for sensible integrated transport policies. Depressingly, the most important reason for changes of policy was money. By the end of 1973, inflation was reaching alarming proportions. The OCR was probably the least cost-effective of all Bristol's poposals. It would never have been built beyond the Three Lamps even if the

Council could have acted faster and by 1972 a crystal ball would have revealed that Stage II would never have been built either.

The Campaign achieved some of its ends, but not all. It raised in the public's mind an awareness of the threat of urban road schemes and helped change the minds of some of the City's political leaders, but not all. It helped pave the way for a saner plan for the Docks, for while the line of the road remained, nothing intelligent could happen there. Its biggest failure was Totterdown where 550 houses were destroyed unnecessarily and the open land there now stands empty – a monument to the passion for change and development which obsessed the Planning Committee in the fifties and sixties.

PART III

THE CHANGING CLIMATE:
The development of participation
Introduction

In the 1970s, consultation became a key word in the planners' vocabulary. The Civic Amenities Act and its chief promoter, the Civic Trust, sprang directly from the need. The Skeffington Report 'People and Planning' laid down an ideal for consultation processes. At the same time the architects – under pressure because after a whole generation of flag waving about the new architecture they had failed to sell it to the public at large, and aware of a growing concern about economy on maintenance and heating – were beginning to think again about traditional materials and traditional forms. There was a revival of interest in the older parts of our cities, whilst restoration was shown as an economically feasible alternative to demolition and rebuilding. In Bristol the first half of the decade was marked by a series of important public inquiries over proposals to demolish old buildings for new, larger ones.

These inquiries saw developers and local authority ranged on one side and the amenity societies on the other. Although the societies had little money, they usually put up sufficiently powerful arguments to win the day. The high success rate in these local inquries may have had some effect on the local authority attitude, although the most important single factor here was the arrival of younger men in the planning office, ready and willing to talk to the amenity lobby.

Open spaces

One important area of planning and environmental concern is that relating to open spaces, and the new readiness to talk and work in harmony, even in partnership, is nowhere more in evidence than here. But it was not always so; since the parks and open spaces have not so far been discussed, the story must begin with a retrospective account of the Bristol open space scene.

Bristol set about its post-war planning aware of the great imbalance in the provision of open space between the north-west of the City (with the Avon Gorge, Clifton and Durdham Downs and Blaise Castle Estate) and the rest. The north-east sector had the Oldbury Court Estate and other areas had their commons (of which six existed in Bristol) and parks. But in 1952 the favoured sector contained nearly half of the 1509 acres of public open space then available.

The City had a responsibility to produce an overall plan for all open space. Aware of the grave deficiencies in the central and eastern parts of the City, and recognising the impossibility of correcting the balance in the inner city areas, it saw the acquisition of open space on the fringes as a means of meeting the needs of the deprived areas. Thus the acquisition in 1960 of the vast Ashton Court Estate was seen as a solution for south-western areas of the City, and provision was made to include a further 220 acres of the old Whitchurch Airport as public open space to serve the south. Another projected fringe 'district open space' was to be in the north-east sector, where the City purchased Wallscourt Farm, adjacent to Lockleaze.

The Development Plan Review of 1966 referred with some pride to two long pedestrian walks through amenity areas which were already in existence: the Trym Valley path from Sea Mills to Coombe Dingle and thence to Penpole Point, Kingsweston, Blaise or Henbury, and the Frome Valley path from Stapleton Bridge through Oldbury Court Estate to Frenchay. It also mentioned the fact that though there were 553 footpaths and bridlepaths in

Bristol, of a total length of 95 miles (182 paths repaired at public expense), this showed a slight reduction on the position at a survey twelve years earlier. There was no statement of intent to do anything specific about footpaths and pedestrians, although the Development Plan itself stated clear objectives for the development of an integrated system of pedestrian ways throughout the City and for the segregation of pedestrians from vehicles. This was, of course, to be achieved as far as the City centre was concerned by vertical segregation, that is, by the provision of a network of decks above the level of the roads and ground. The emphasis in planning documents of the 1960s was on vehicles and roads.

The purchase of the Ashton Court Estate was of major significance. For the sum of £103,200 Bristol acquired 840 acres of land, and with it, a large house, put together gradually over the centuries from the fourteenth to the nineteenth and containing in the great south-west wing the first Palladian building in Bristol sometimes, perhaps wishfully, attributed to Inigo Jones. The house showed all the signs of neglect following its war service, and it smelt strongly of dry rot. With the estate came also gardens, farmbuildings and woodlands. The City already owned and managed other estates – notably the 191 acres of Blaise and the 115 acre Oldbury Court. But it had noting on the scale of Ashton Court and its major problems of building restoration and estate reorganisation and management.

At first, the City seemed to do nothing, except produce nasty signs and inappropriately placed car parks. However, the Society for the Preservation of Ancient Bristol moved rapidly. They commissioned Donald Insall to produce a report which in June 1960 they sent to the Lord Mayor. The first paragraph relating to the estate reads:

'The grounds of Ashton Court will now inevitably find increasing demands for uses and development of all kinds; and some form of planned policy for the whole area is first an urgent necessity. . . . The first necessity is to prepare a comprehensive survey upon which a firm detailed policy can be established for the Estate, its development and management. . . . The survey

75

should analyse in detail the agricultural and recreational assets of the Estate, its differential land values and demands.'

The report went on to make a strong recommendation that a special body responsible to the Council should be charged with the duty of forming an initial policy for the estate and administering its more immediate problems 'so that sight is not lost of the wider issues and possibilities'.

The *Bristol Forum Journal* advocated the setting up of a special committee, a 'design and research group', consisting of landscape architect, forestry advisers, consultant engineers and architects and representatives of the various Corporation Departments concerned with the future of the estate. Its function would be to determine the detailed uses of the estate and draw up plans to implement these.

By the following summer, some forty-eight acres of pasture land were being converted for organised games and an old army hut was being erected for dressing rooms; a pitch and putt course had been made (another to follow later) and discussions were in progress with the University and the Education Committee concerning the use of land for playing fields. An overall plan? A survey?

By the next summer, there was talk of an open-air lido, indoor bowling greens and even the building of a new College of Art in the grounds, whilst suggestions for the house included a conference centre, carriage museum and a student hall of residence. An overall plan? A survey? Even a committee with special responsibility to formulate these?

Bristol Civic Society pressed consistently in correspondence and in the press for a plan to be drawn up, pointing to the alarming likelihood that in its absence the estate would gradually be filled with uses suggested by the more persuasive sections of the community, not because Ashton Court was the best place for them, but simply because it seemed to be there for the asking. The Society also supported the proposal for a special committee to deal with the problems of development of the estate, suggesting that profits could be ploughed back directly into the maintenance of the park and its woodlands. It cited the bold decision, in 1961, to set up a separate committee to administer the Downs, since triumphantly vindicated.

By 1964, permission had been granted for the installation of a small-bore rifle range and 'consideration will continually be given to the introduction of such items as bowling greens, tennis courts, cricket squares, children's playgrounds and the like . . . dependent upon the finances being available . . .' (City Engineer in a letter to Bristol Chamber of Commerce). Still no plan. A full size golf-course and a caravan park were also seriously considered.

In 1966, the Planning Committee received a proposal for a £200,000 scheme for the conversion of the house (including a new ballroom built on at the back) for use as an assembly room and banqueting complex, but felt it could not proceed because of lack of funds. Over the years there had been talks between the Civic Society and the Bristol Chamber of Commerce, and in July 1968 they went together to the City to offer to promote a Public Fund to get work on the house in motion; the offer was not accepted. The Bristol Society of Architects made similar attempts.

At last, in 1971, a Ball proposed by the Bristol Society of Architects had to be put off because the house could no longer be declared safe; the consequent publicity and public pressure caused the Council to promote an architectural competition and the scheme put forward by Whicheloe Macfarlane Partnership in association with Tolson and Goldsmith was selected. Work began in 1974 and, four years later, Bristolians rejoiced to see and enjoy the rooms restored and opened for their use. But the estate as a whole? Was it part of the plan? Or of any plan?

The Civic Society has repeatedly drawn attention over Ashton Court to the situation in which the City found itself – something comparable to that of the National Trust – where it was seeking to plan and manage an historic estate, including general landscape, woodlands and buildings, designed originally for the use of one family, and now to be open to use and enjoyment by thousands of families. To create as well as to preserve – to originate in the context of conservation – called for professional expertise of a specialised kind, not normally found or needed before in local government.

This need was nowhere more apparent than in the Blaise Castle Estate in the latter part of the 1970s. Again, there is no overall plan and, although the land has been well administered as a public park, it has been allowed to deteriorate very severely as an historic landscape and as woodland. In its woodlands, Dutch elm disease and the beech bark disease enhanced by the 1977 drought accentuated the disaster. Over the years, isolated areas were planted with young trees, but thinning and general attention was minimal. The tendency to rely for the rest on natural regeneration has failed because most young trees are decapitated and stripped by the squirrels which abound. Officially sponsored orienteering leads to general 'adventure playground' use of the woodland slopes, effectively removing ground cover, and making the exposed soil prone to erosion and landslip. The oldest part of the estate, Blaise Castle Folly, predating Humphrey Repton's reorganisation of the park, was incorporated into the new layout to make the focus of an important vista from the house, but has now been planted around and is hardly visible; it is also a ruin. As at Ashton Court there has been a gradual introduction of putting, miniature railway, children's playground, 'trim-track', without any overall plan.

The Civic Society was not the only body – or even perhaps the first – to urge that the City should equip itself to deal effectively with its open spaces. Back in 1962–63, the New Bristol Group, in its publication *Outlook*, recommended that a new committee be set up, independent of the Planning and Public Works Committee which tagged parks along behind all its other responsibilities, which would advise on the allocation of land for parks and open spaces, formulate development policies and administer existing parks and open spaces. It also urged that a chief officer should be appointed. It was not, however, to be until April 1974 that the City established an Open Spaces and Amenities Committee, and not until 1979 that a separate Parks Department, with its own chief officer responsible to the Open Spaces and Amenities Committee, was created.

The new Committee leapt into action in July 1974, with the production of a 'Green Paper' on *Recreation and Amenity* which set out the facilities available and the expenditure currently incurred on them. It is significant that the main emphasis was on sport and the provision of sports and play facilities. There was no reference to the maintenance of historic estates and woodlands or to pro-

Ashton Court's superb landscape grown old; its new use as a city park creates problems not yet resolved.

An unusual view of the magnificent restoration of Ashton Court House.

posals to draw up plans for them. The emphasis seemed to be on the needs of the young, rather than of whole families.

Nevertheless, the planning of sports facilities poses real problems in terms of appropriate treatment and access for all who need them. The Bristol Sports Association had approved a draft paper on planning for sport in Bristol emphasising the need for an indoor multi-sports centre; the need for a municipal golf course, a tartan athletics track, a cycling track, a ski-slope and a floodlit all-weather soccer/hockey pitch was also emphasised.

A Sports Liaison Council composed of equal numbers of City Council members and Sports Association representatives was formed in 1969 after three years of pressure from the Sports Association. At its first meeting plans were produced for a golf course at Ashton Court and a cinder 400-metre track at Netham. The Sports Association pressed for an indoor sports centre as top priority and emphasised the importance of planning for multi-sports centres rather than building separate facilities. The early years were characterised by a lack of mutual understanding which was not helped by the Council's continued habit of making decisions and plans without consultation. The break-through came with the decision to convert a hangar at Whitchurch into a multi-sports centre; co-operation over this project paved the way for a better understanding and working relationship.

Bristol Sports Association also played a significant part in the Golden Hill Playing Fields inquiry. Together with the Sports Council they objected to the request for planning permission, by the YMCA and Bristol Grammar School, to sell the land for housing development. Loss of recreational land within the City centre was seen as part of the general erosion of open space within cities, and it was revealed that the Council had no recreational plan for the City. The outcome of the inquiry, with the Grammar School land remaining for recreational use, was highly satisfactory.

It is interesting to see how many of the Sports Association's recommendations have been achieved in the past ten years. Bristol now has two major Sports Centres, at Whitchurch and Kingsdown, and the first of a series of neighbourhood Sports Centres at Easton; there is a regional tartan athletics track at Whitchurch and a cycle track in Hengrove Park; the plans for a golf course are still on ice. In addition there is a temporary Water Leisure Centre at Baltic Wharf in the City Docks and the prospect of further development for water sports at the Albion Dockyard.

The new arrangement whereby Bristol has an Indoor Recreation Manager, a Parks Manager and an officer from the City Engineer's Department in charge of the City Docks augurs well for the future.

A new park for which the Open Spaces and Amenities Committee took over responsibility – to the strains of the City of Bristol Band, at its opening ceremony in 1978 – was Castle Park on the site of Bristol's all-but-vanished castle. The birth pangs of this struggling infant had been protracted, and it finally entered the world at a time of great financial strain, not at all the lusty offspring which had been planned. The official City Centre Policy Report of 1966 showed the area bounded by High Street, Wine Street and Lower Castle Street to be developed in the terms of a scheme put forward by consultants Sir Hugh Casson, Neville Condor & Partners in 1962. This provided for a new museum and art gallery bounding two sides of a new St. Peter's Square (retaining the ruins of the bombed St. Peter's Church), an arts centre to the east and, beyond that, on the section adjoining Lower Castle Street, a park incorporating the remains of the castle banqueting hall (the vaulted chamber) and the old City wall. By Bristol Bridge, a small riverside hotel and restaurant were proposed, and to the north-west a block for cultural, professional and exhibition purposes.

The consultants had been commissioned following the furore in the previous year when it was discovered that the grand proposal designating the area a new civic centre contained in the 1956 Development Plan had been quietly eroded, and that the City had leased key sites to the Norwich Union Insurance Company and the Bank of England. But although they had been commissioned, the consultants had not been clearly briefed as to resources available and the resulting £$\frac{1}{4}$ million scheme they produced eventually proved too expensive.

Gradually the concept of a grand civic centre evaporated and its potential users began to look elsewhere. Then it was decided to use the whole area for a park, a really splendid park – an open space in the southern part of the City centre where open space is

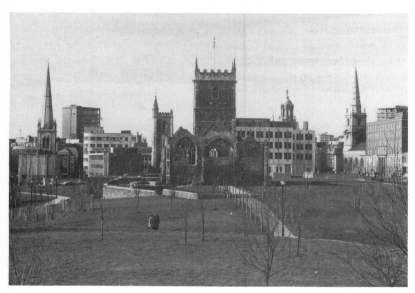

Castle Park in the making.

scarce. Casson produced another plan, which made imaginative use of the area, retaining and enhancing the remains of the castle and the ruins of St. Peter's, and incorporating a variety of features including a Palm House, and ranging from formal layouts for herb garden and water garden and avenues of trees to informal stretches of grass, trees and children's play area. No decision was made and costs continued to rise. Finally, in 1977, work began on an emasculated version of the plan, revised not by the consultants but by the Parks Department. The Civic Society pressed consistently for adherence to the scheme itself, with implementation as funds became available, and asked that at least options should be kept open to create the park as conceived by its designer. For the most part, the park which emerged does this where it does not actually incorporate the proposed features.

In the following year, Bristol could congratulate itself on having actually opened a new City centre park (although incomplete) in one of the worst years of financial doldrums. But it took sixteen years to reach a point where it could be opened at all. The intervening years were marked by the most astonishing delays in which the price escalated from £¼ million to over £1 million, much more than the original cost of the whole Civic Centre project.

If the 1960s were the years of the road and the motor car, the 1970s gave some prominence to the pedestrian, most clearly illustrated in the national fever for the production of 'trails'. Bristol has not fallen behind in the walking race, and numerous organisations have produced maps, booklets and routes based on existing footpaths. One important achievement of the later 1970s was the creation by Bristol Corporation (largely from existing footpaths, and with the help of the Job Creation Scheme) of the Avon Walkway. This stemmed from an idea put forward in one of the lively *Twenty Ideas for Bristol* exhibitions in the City Museum. The new feel for the significance of the pedestrian in the modern city seemed to be symbolised by the realisation that the Bristolian could actually walk from Pill to the City Centre almost without setting foot on a road (or pavement alongside one), and that he could continue in like manner to Conham, or up through St. Anne's Park to Brislington. On occasions the City is slow to celebrate its achievements. So it was left to the Civic Society to publicise this new pedestrian way by producing a map leaflet and by organising (on a wet summer's evening) a grand opening ceremony with groups of people from a range of amenity societies as well as councillors and officers walking along the route from all directions and converging on a waterside park little known to any of them, Spark Evans Park, for the official opening.

This was the first major pedestrian route to be created in the City for many years, the Trym and Frome paths having long existed. Proposals began to emerge for others. Most ambitious was the joint Cyclebag and Pedestrians Association scheme for a foot and cycle path from Old Market to Bitton, making use of existing paths and creating new links. Cyclebag, a group dedicated to the promotion of cycling as a means of transport and recreation, was making Bristolians aware of cyclists and their needs. In February 1979, a farseeing policy document was prepared by the City Planning Officer making both a general case for the need for a detailed policy and specific immediate priorities for the provision of routes for cyclists.

Tree planting on the quayside.

The co-operative spirit between City and amenity societies which set up the Avon Walkway was increasingly a feature of the 1970s. This kind of co-operation is best exemplified by the scheme for the planting of trees in Bristol's streets. In 1973, the national 'Plant a Tree' year, a Tree Planting Year Appeal Fund had been set up jointly by the Bristol Society of Architects (whose idea it was), the Conservation Society, the Arboricultural Association, the Gloucestershire Branch of the Council for the Preservation of Rural England and the Bristol Civic Society, its area covering the West Country and South Wales. Since its manpower was largely Bristol-based, it is not surprising that most of the earmarked sums contributed came from the Bristol area, and at the end of the year the Civic Society agreed to promote the venture on a continuing basis. The result was the Bristol Civic Society Tree Appeal Fund. Whereas in a rural area the success of tree planting schemes depends on the co-operation of private landowners, large and small, a city scheme stands or falls on the attitude of the local authority. The Bristol scheme was blessed from the start, and the interest, commitment and involvement of the Planning Department and of the Parks Department in Bristol has been exceptional. A group, at which officers have been present, has met regularly to discuss the choice of sites and species for planting as well as to evolve the general policies for the use of the funds. The trees are paid for by the public through the Fund, and are planted and maintained by the Corporation. The Fund has formed the channel through which individuals and organisations can arrange and contribute towards tree planting in their area, and other amenity societies, notably Clifton and Hotwells Improvement Society and the Redland and Cotham Amenities Society, have played an active part in the group's work.

Some 800 trees had been planted in the streets of Bristol, mostly in the City centre and key arterial road sites, between 1973 and the end of the 79/80 winter planting season. Only a small proportion were replacements, reflecting an early policy decision to buy and plant mainly extra heavy standard trees, found by experience to be much more proof against vandals than cheaper, younger specimens. Many miles of streets remain to be planted, but the steady progress made is substantial, with the establishment of street tree planting as a regular part of the City's programme. A glance at the City Engineer's Report for 1962–63 – when the total number of street trees in Bristol actually declined during the year by thirty-seven – underlines the shift of values.

To a smaller extent, the Fund also involved itself in bulb planting. The cheerful banks of daffodils which now bloom in the spring under the multi-storey car park on The Triangle and on four sites on the edges of Castle Park facing the end of Merchant Street were planted in holes dug by the Parks Department by members of the public who bought their bulb through the Fund, any surplus received going to pay for more street trees. Such a partnership patently works where there is a specific task to be performed and a common purpose to see it accomplished. It could perhaps serve as a model for other schemes in a future of scarce material and monetary resources.

An 'offshoot' of the tree-planting scheme, and one which it is hoped will pay double dividends, is the establishment of tree nurseries in a number of Bristol schools through the enthusiasm and commitment of a small group of teachers. In this way, a stock of young trees will be acquired cheaply for planting out on derelict open space in a few years' time. More important, perhaps, is the interest and involvement of the young people concerned.

Despite very substantial progress, the underlying need – stressed repeatedly by the Civic Society and others – for an overall policy for the City's parks and open spaces remains unmet. Without such a policy, improvements here and there may be individually excellent, but they may ultimately be stultifying or prove to be wasted. Within an overall policy, detailed plans for each of the parks, especially the major ones, need to be worked out. The wide range of uses for public parks, as for water space, can be conflicting, but conflict can be minimised by careful planning built on consultation.

In spite of the continued absence of any general open space policy or plans, certain new developments in the form of major urban fringe projects at Hartcliffe, Lawrence Weston and Stockwood are being pursued by the Corporation, following an initiative by the Countryside Commission.

Unfortunately, there seems to be no current policy for the

posed public open space at Wallscourt Farm and the surrounding land; there is an urgent need for an overall plan here, before more land is used for other purposes.

One specific matter stressed by the Civic Society is the special kind of overall management policy and detailed planning required for areas of woodland. Detailed plans are required specifying the planting, thinning and felling sequence to be followed for a particular area over the years. The life cycle of a woodland is thus treated as a continuous process and sudden changes in the landscape are avoided. The initial policy within which such detailed plans are drawn up will have laid down broad principles, such as whether an historic landscape should be replanted to its original design, and whether and to what extent the woodland should be treated as a commercial proposition with sale of timber.

In 1979, the City took an important step, setting up a Woodland Advisory Consultative Committee and appointing a consultant forester to make a survey of the current state of the woodlands in the City's ownership. Such positive steps constitute a major change in direction and attitude, and should mean that such money as is available to be spent on the City's woodlands will be put to constructive use within an overall policy and plan.

New uses for old buildings

Our attitude to old buildings has changed radically over the last few years. In 1966, the Great Western Cotton Mill, beside the feeder canal at Barton Hill, was demolished with horrifying economy and precision by one man and a machine. This great building was, perhaps, the best example of large scale nineteenth century industrial building in the City: now it has completely gone, and is replaced with single storeyed industrial sheds. In 1966, demolition went relatively unheeded; today this mill would almost certainly be rescued and re-used. It was a multi-storeyed structure in reasonable condition, with vast usable spaces contained within a substantial masonry shell, accessible by canal, and easily by road. Had it survived, it would have given architectural distinction and imagery to the area, now an architectural wasteland.

Fortunately, the climate of opinion has changed, and Bristol can now offer many examples of intelligent re-use of existing buildings. Much work has been sponsored or achieved by the City, and much by private enterprise. Sadly, some worthwhile structures still disappear, but less frequently.

The re-use of buildings like Quakers' Friars, revived as Register Office and Town Planning Exhibition, and the former Merchants' Almshouses, now Lloyds Bank, demonstrates an early and enlightened realisation in Bristol of the value derived from recycling existing buildings which have outlived an original function. It is sad that, in Quakers' Friars, the opportunity was not then seized of turning the shops towards the old building group, which could have provided an attractive traffic-free shopping square.

But the major thrust has been more recent, especially in the last ten years or so. There have been various factors: public appreciation, awakened by the amenity societies, of the positive virtues of renewal; increasingly effective legislation in such measures as the Civic Amenities Act and the designation of conservation areas; the bursting of the office-boom bubble; even, sad to admit, general dislike of modern buildings, transferred to a popular preference for old buildings rather than new in almost any circumstance. The results of this reassessment of values can be seen in a wide variety of building conversions or rehabilitations in Bristol. Argument will no doubt continue as to the economic soundness of re-use, although the value of maintaining old buildings as a substantial part of the fabric of cities is hard to quantify. The large numbers of re-used buildings makes it clear that there is a growing appreciation of the value of continued and adaptive use: the solid structure and spaciousness of many older structures are both difficult to provide at present costs. These factors, added to the advantage of established central sites, make for sound sense in adaptation. It is only quite recently that the notion of putting up buildings for an immediate limited life only has developed, just as we limit (unnecessarily) the life of our motor cars. Our older schools demonstrate how relatively easy it is to adapt new methods to existing buildings, and in the process the surroundings often become richer than they might otherwise be. The Victorian schools of Bristol might sometimes lack full modern amenities, but they do have qualities of space, detailed interest and fine workmanship which it was not possible to achieve in post-war schools.

With the closure of the City Docks to normal commerce, many of the specialist service buildings erected there in the nineteenth century have become redundant, and here some imaginative conversions have been or are about to be made. Deservedly best known is the great Bush Warehouse now used by the Arnolfini (and occupying its third consecutive rehabilitated ware-house) together with suites of offices in grand rooms with generous central service areas, and the architects' own offices in the new glazed roof storey. This was an instance where the outer shell only could be kept, the interior being restructured in reinforced concrete. The original interior was not of a sufficiently unique or forceful character to warrant retention, at high cost and inconvenience to the new use, although generally it is happier if at least some part of the original structuring can be retained to be seen in the new work. The exterior, now so finely cleaned and refurbished, is one of the most impressive parts of the Bristol waterfront. Demolition would have been disastrous, yet the City Development Plan (including the

Quakers' Friars: the old buildings well converted to new uses, but unimaginative planning has left them in a nasty backyard rather than the town square that might have been.

1966 Review) showed the northern two bays of this building swept away to make way for a road. It is heartening to see the recently restored Edward Gabriel's 'E' Shed, with its memorable domed corner facing the Centre, being prepared for use as an Arts Centre, and, equally exciting, to learn that, in addition to the impressive WCA Warehouse, the two halves of the dramatic Buchanan's Wharf warehouse – opposite the Old Granary – may be rescued for use by a housing association. These massive brick structures are especially worth keeping because of the fine way in which they rise direct from the water's edge, Venice-like, while offering accommodation in the heart of the City, with magnificent panoramic views from the upper storeys.

The City Museum has adapted one of the transit sheds on the south side of the river for use as an Industrial Museum and a Royal National Lifeboat Institute museum is also planned for this site. In St. Augustine's Reach, a private concern has opened an

Exhibition Centre in the early twentieth century concrete framed sheds opposite the Bush building. Finally, the lowest storeys of the Old Granary – architecturally of equal quality, though quite different in character from the Bush warehouse – have for a number of years housed a club. One hopes that this extraordinary 'Bristol Byzantine' building with its uniquely varied brick detailing will one day be more fully used: it has a most enticing roof space, two storeys high, which calls out to be the most splendid penthouse dwelling in the south-west, and several intermediate floors now standing empty. The building illustrates many of the problems which beset the designer on conversion jobs: low ceiling heights; difficult fire escape; timber floor structure (unique in its treatment of the floor joists). But with zeal and good will these snags can be overcome, and the Old Granary must eventually be fully used, if possible, including retention of at least one floor to remind us of its interesting formation.

Standing high above the water at the top of the red cliff, the row of houses in Redcliffe Parade, built just two hundred years ago, has been revived to create a dignified piece of townscape. Most are no longer private houses, and the restored and redecorated facades conceal a set of office spaces engineered within the old rooms, incorporated with a large, completely new extension on the south side, hardly seen from the old city area. This particular piece of refurbishment illustrates the possibilities of 'conservation gain' which can be organised by fruitful discussion between developers and planners. The developer gets his large extra areas of floor in return for putting cash and energy into restoring the old buildings, and the City retains a valuable part of its heritage. Of a different order, the terrace of town houses forming the east side of Park Place once threatened with demolition is now fully restored and uses include both government offices and private apartments. To a large extent the decision to rehabilitate rather than to rebuild here was conditioned by public reaction; as a consequence this attractive little urban space, tucked in behind Maples, still has buildings of an appropriate scale bounding its edges.

In Brunswick Square, the 'palace front' row of houses on the south side, now and for many years sadly in decline, was the object of a Public Inquiry in which the Civic Society, with others,

Three imposing dockside warehouses: WCA and Buchanan's Wharf on Redcliffe Backs awaiting restoration and conversion to housing; and the famous Old Granary long since converted to use as a jazz club.

The Old Granary: Bristol Byzantine detail.

pleaded successfully for the retention of these elegant buildings – in scale with the eighteenth century square – for new use as offices. This seemed a pyrrhic victory, but at the time of writing, a restoration project is firmly timetabled in the City's conservation programme for which Central Government funds should be available.

Portland Square – in many ways the finest of all Bristol's eighteenth century domestic layouts, particularly when one takes into account the related streets – is at last beginning to look worth visiting again. It has had a long and degrading history of new use, with grand mansions used as factories, warehouses and doss-houses and with large, untidy signs spread over the handsome Bath stone facades. Years of pressure from planners and amenity societies is now paying off, but during the great office boom developers too often got away with that least desirable of conservation techniques, the grafting of new buildings onto the old facades. A disastrous fire, completely destroying the Salvation Army Hostel, has set back progress; but a number of other schemes about to start will bring back some residential accommodation into the area and help pull Portland Square fully out of its hundred year old eclipse.

On the grandest scale of domestic work, the mansion of Ashton Court, owned by the City since 1960, is at long last being given a new lease of life. Fifteen years ago such a resuscitation must have seemed extremely unlikely to all but the most optimistic. The building illustrates another of the dilemmas of re-use – finding an appropriate and beneficial function; if a structure is to be maintained because it has architectural or historic validity, meaningful use must be established in order to justify costs of rehabilitation and expense of continued maintenance.

There is great concern for the future of Kingsweston House. The City Planning Committee, after taking note of very strong local and amenity society objections, rejected the detailed and architecturally attractive proposals to build the Avon and Somerset Police Headquarters close to the Mansion. The Police Authority is currently seeking other sites but, in a remarkable initiative, the City Planning Office have recently produced a guideline scheme that would allow the police to develop on the site, leave the

Mansion free-standing as the important monument that it is, allocate part of the grounds as public open space, all whilst allowing the police to remain in the house and thus continue to act as its protectors. This could be and should be the ideal solution to a most difficult conservation dilemma.

The sad loss of the whole interior of St. Nicholas' Church through bombing nevertheless presented an opportunity which has been well exploited. Here the City has rebuilt the interior to provide a first class Ecclesiastical Museum and Museum of Local History, combined with a brass rubbing centre, recital room, and meeting space, so that the building is again much used, while remaining a consecrated church, with the crypt as chapel. At the time of writing, the Diocese is waiting to hear from the Church Commissioners about proposals to make a series of other central churches redundant. Should this happen, ingenuity will be needed to find suitable new uses. There are many examples in Britain and other parts of the world demonstrating the feasibility of careful and valuable re-use, and already one Bristol building of major significance in architectural history – the former Highbury Chapel (William Butterfield's very first design) – has been reorganised for use as the Anglican parish church for Cotham. This is a reorganisation rather than re-use perhaps, but a better new use than the furniture warehouse which at one time seemed likely.

In contrast, the splendid little brick church of St. Gabriel, Easton – which could so easily have been transformed into a valuable community asset as library, youth centre or community centre, with a minimum of additional work to the building – has been demolished. It was the only truly memorable building in that area of new housing, with an interior of breath-taking quality. Another space in danger is the Unitarian Chapel in Lewins Mead. Now much too big to be supported by its greatly diminished congregation, the building was to be swept away and replaced by another multi-storeyed office block, but both popular opposition and the lessening of commercial pressures have given this a reprieve; once again, it is vital that a continuing use be found for this building. In the meantime, some modest maintenance expenditure could ensure that it does not deteriorate whilst waiting for rebirth.

An early lithograph of Brunel's great train shed at Temple Meads. Its restoration as an exhibition hall is the most likely new use.

As a final illustration of the opportunities for reorganisation of buildings, and of the flexibilities offered, a glance along King Street – perhaps the best of Bristol's streets – shows how much has already been achieved: warehouses into offices and restaurants, a great eighteenth century trade hall as foyer to the theatre, the first City Library as restaurant. Interestingly, the two sets of almshouses are among the few buildings of any age in original use.

There will continue to be opportunities for intelligent appraisal of old buildings leading to renewal of life in them. A major historic structure, of national interest, even now under review by British Rail, is Brunel's train shed and offices at Temple Meads: used for some years as a car park (better in itself than demolition), it is beginning to look drab and somewhat tattered, and one can perhaps sympathise with the owners who have to try to maintain it at high annual cost. However, quite recently, after years of amenity society pressure, British Rail have grasped the nettle, commissioned an architect to prepare feasibility studies for active and gainful new use, and given grounds for hope of a satisfactory solution.

Conservation programme

In 1974, the commercial property market collapsed. Developers, many of whom had paid enormously inflated prices for sites with office planning permissions, found their properties worth a fraction of values a year before, whilst building costs began to soar. There were millions of square feet of unlet offices, built during the boom, with no tenants in sight.

At the same time, public opinion was running against the relentless destruction not only of individual buildings of character, but of the very fabric of the City. In particular feelings ran high against the plans for new roads which had formed part of the Bristol Development Plan for many years. Participation was the slogan in planning, and as has been seen, the one clear message given by the people who lived in areas affected, such as Totterdown and St. Paul's, was that they did not want the Outer Circuit Road, which probably threatened more historic buildings than any other single project.

Before April 1st, 1974, the Bristol Planning Committee had responsibility for highways, as well as for all other planning matters. Under local government reorganisation, Avon County Council took over responsibility for highways and transport, as well as all strategic planning.

Bristol was now restricted to control of new development on a site by site basis, and to small scale planning matters. The highway engineers mostly moved to Avon. They were no longer 'in house'; they no longer had the first word. This may be thought an over-simplification and, to some extent it is, but the change in responsibility was important for a department which, until 1972, was the City Engineer and Planning Officer's Department headed by an engineer, rather than by an architect planner.

The outlook at this time was grim indeed. Large stretches of the inner city were derelict, with buildings either demolished or empty and decaying. Almost all commercial activity had ceased in the City Docks, with no clear policy for the use of the vast area

98

of land thereby released. At the same time the national economy was in recession, with virtually no money available publicly or privately for development.

The main hope for conservationists was that the dearth of funds would, at the least, cause a substantial slowdown in demolitions. With no funds for building work, there was no incentive to buy property, or to demolish buildings already bought. In view of the repeated successes of the amenity societies at public inquiries the message gradually got through that applications for demolition consent were invariably expensive for developers and usually unsuccessful. Some were withdrawn; the flow of new applications slowed.

In the second half of the seventies there was steady and accelerating progress in dealing with the legacy of destruction and neglect. Prior to 1974 only six conservation areas had been designated; Henbury, Westbury, Stapleton, Clifton, the City and Queen Square and Kingsdown. In the second half of that year, and the first half of 1975, a further six areas were designated; St. Michael's Hill and Christmas Steps, Portland Square, Park Street and Brandon Hill, College Green, Shirehampton and Redcliffe. Four more areas have since been designated; Montpelier, Whiteladies Road, Old Market and the City Docks.

Conservation area protection meant that permission to demolish any building, whether 'listed' or not, had to be obtained. It also meant that the local authority could demand higher standards of design in areas that were specifically classified as of architectural importance. Finally, central government grants became available for buildings in 'outstanding' conservation areas. Clifton, and the City and Queen Square were already so classified. Since 1974, such classification has been obtained for Portland Square, St. Michael's Hill and Christmas Steps, Park Street and Brandon Hill and College Green.

By the end of the summer of 1975 the number of conservation areas in the City had been doubled. This helped to stop demolition but did little to revitalise the City Centre; decay and dereliction were still unchecked. In the autumn of 1975, however, the City Council appointed a new City Planning Officer, Jim Preston, who, in the short period of eighteen months before his death, made a tremendous impact on planning in Bristol and set off a number of initiatives which began to remedy the decay, and to conserve Bristol's heritage. Many of his initiatives were to launch and push schemes and policies that had been worked on and put into drawers in the Planning Office over a long period. Mr. Preston 'made things happen' in a way that enlivened his colleagues and, for the first time in Bristol, made planning a positive process.

During 1976 a pedestrianisation scheme for Corn Street was implemented and the area was paved to a high standard with pennant stone. A start was made in removing car parking from Welsh Back and plans were prepared for a paving scheme in Narrow Quay and, again, the removal of car parking. The groundwork was also done in preparing for a full scale study of the problems and opportunities presented by the City Docks after the virtual ending of commercial use. The study proceeded during 1977, but at the same time planning briefs were prepared for several sites in the Docks thought suitable for early release. Such briefs were also prepared and published on other key sites in the City, setting out the criteria by which the Planning Committee would judge any application for planning permission. A common enough planning procedure, but the opening of such matters to public discussion was new in Bristol. Also during 1976, the City Planners began to face up to the problems of dereliction, about which they had been prodded and nagged for so long by amenity societies. A survey of derelict buildings was put in hand.

By April 1977 the City Planning Department was able to demonstrate to its committee how derelict buildings exacerbated the problems of the inner city. The officers pointed out, with great tact, that many decaying, listed buildings were owned by the Council and that if the City could see its way to finding money for restoration, grants would be available from the Department of the Environment.

This was in effect the beginning of the City's five-year conservation programme. The Committee and its officers worked with tremendous speed, and by November 1977 had committed Bristol to a five-year programme of grant-aided restoration of historic buildings in the City Centre. Bristol was to contribute £100,000 a year and the Historic Buildings Council, which

100

Freeland Place: part conservation and part 'new build' to provide a replacement for the old Rownham Inn. Prince Street: a former merchant's house whose exterior has been restored to its former glory now provides accommodation for three families.

101

allocates the Department of the Environment grants, promised a similar sum. In the case of property owned by the local authority or housing associations, the grant would be 50 per cent of the cost of the conservation element of any scheme; further substantial sums would come from housing funds for the 'housing element'. In the case of private developers, the grant was normally to be 25 per cent. Although the total of £200,000 per year would not buy a great deal of building work, the programme was essentially a 'pump-priming' exercise, the aim being to generate enthusiasm and optimism and to persuade other owners to improve their properties.

In 1977/78, the first year of the programme, five schemes were approved, and by 1980, were all completed or virtually complete.

1. *1 and 1a Christmas Steps.* Refurbishment of two superb buildings, in a totally derelict state and a prominent eyesore for many years.
2. *66 Prince Street.* Rehabilitation for housing of a splendid eighteenth century merchant's house.
3. *78/100 St. Michael's Hill.* Restoration of a terrace of Georgian houses in the BRI precinct, for hostel accommodation.
4. *19 Freeland Place.* Restoration and completion in period style of a nintheenth century terrace truncated by road widening.
5. *Further paving in Welsh Back and Narrow Quay.*

In 1978/79, the City increased the programme out of all recognition. It first of all obtained an increased 'normal' allocation of grant (£160,000) from the Historic Buildings Council. Then, when further funds became available as part of government's efforts to stimulate the economy, it obtained an additional grant of £236,483. This was a very considerable achievement since this last figure was offered in September 1978, and was available only for schemes which could be completed by April 1979, a very short time-scale.

By early 1980, with the five-year programme having reached the half-way stage, its results can be seen on the ground, and in the

Superb restoration at the foot of Christmas Steps after a decade of dereliction. This first phase of a much larger project included the conversion of a pennant stone warehouse in nearby Host Street for Bristol Old Vic.

further proposals it has stimulated. Narrow Quay has been re-paved and 'E' Shed made safe and restored externally, giving a new vitality to St. Augustine's Reach. At the other end of the Centre, 1 and 1a Christmas Steps at last make a worthy termination to the steps, and the nearby warehouse in Host Street has been rebuilt as a furniture store for the Bristol Old Vic.

Essential to the success of the Conservation Programme has been the co-operation of the City Council's Housing Committee and of the housing associations active in Bristol. In areas where refurbishment for commercial use is not viable, housing funds have been essential. Lodge Street, 66 Prince Street, Surrey Lodge, 78–100 St. Michael's Hill, are all residential schemes. The reintroduction of homes to the City centre has wider implications than mere funding. It is part of the general movement to revitalise the inner city, giving it life in the evening as well as during the day, enabling people to live nearer their jobs and the amenities of the City centre.

103

Two further initiatives of the planners involve the reintroduction of residential uses to areas previously zoned for commerce. In the St. Paul's Conservation Area, instead of the previous Development Plan's rigid zoning for commercial use, a range of uses is now proposed including office, residential and some light industry. In Old Market Street similar aims have been pursued by different means, owing to the different form of the problem. In this case the City Planning Committee appointed consultants to make proposals for a large area on the north side of the street. These included a large area of new housing at the rear of a restored historic frontage, to be carried out with the co-operation of Bristol Municipal Charities, the main landowner in the area. Again, conservation grants will be essential for the restoration works.

Little has been said of the role of amenity societies in all this. Their continuous agitation and activity was crucial in the early years, in awakening the public to the value of Bristol's historic architecture, and to the extent of the threat. Without their efforts – in the press, in letters to the planning authority and at public inquiries – the change of heart might well have come too late.

Today, the 'them and us' feeling has given way to consultation and discussion. The Conservation Advisory Panel, set up in January 1977, is a demonstration of this. It is perhaps the most effective outcome of the change in attitude between the Planning Committee and the amenity societies. Although its role is only advisory it provides a forum at which councillors, officials and amenity society representatives work out common attitudes to major planning issues and applications. There is a preponderance of amenity society members and chairmanship is vested in the Civic Society representative. Agenda for meetings are worked out by officials in association with amenity society members. The panel is constituted and functions in such a way that there is no danger that councillors or officials lead the societies towards decisions.

There are still areas of disagreement between the amenity societies and the planners. Limited resources and the enormous backlog of neglect are bound to create differences of view on priorities. Planners have to weigh many considerations in addition to the claims of conservation. But there has been a transformation from the position fifteen years ago.

Urban renewal

It seems a very short time since 'urban renewal' and 'comprehensive development' were thought of as synonymous. As it turned out, the architectural dreams behind the latter proved to be largely unattainable and the effects of the concepts of big scale redevelopment meant big scale urban decay particularly when development ideas were related, as they frequently were, to traffic schemes. In fact, the concept of traffic flowing freely through city centres rebuilt *en bloc* was the dream of the great Swiss architect Le Corbusier in the 1920s which inspired both the planners and architects of the post war era in Britain. The dream required inspired control; indeed, it needed Corbusier himself. Neither was available. In any case, the dream had no basis in social need. The dreamers remained isolated in their belief that a new social order would need new surroundings.

In Britain not even the New Towns achieved a quality that came near to the dream. Rising costs and penny pinching budgets often blinkered the architects' vision, and only at the end of the first post war building phase did anything near the dream materialise. The Barbican in the City of London is an isolated monument which shows that when money, will and inspiration coincide the 'comprehensive' idea works. Mostly it did not work; the result was Broadmead, Lewins Mead and their like all over Britain and then great areas of decay, in storage or ripening, in estate agents terms, for development or road works.

Recognition of the need for urban renewal came late to most cities, as money for the urban motorways ran out. In many ways it was a grass roots movement, not only by young professionals moving back into elegant but decaying areas like Clifton and Hotwells but, a little later, by Indian and West Indian families moving into cheap housing in St. Paul's and similar areas. Faster than the authorities could clear and rehouse, tenants, not wanting to be 'dispersed' into the new suburbs, began to buy from their landlords. Changes in ownership patterns were demonstrated in a

Orchard Street houses which have passed into commercial life rather well.

way that offended the sensibilities of some of the white-skinned natives who were shocked by the cheery, raucous colour schemes chosen to demonstrate take-over, as house after house changed from slovenly rented to family ownership.

This movement has not been properly recognised for what it is, real community-generated renewal which in fact preceded the excellent work that has since been done in the inner suburbs. St. Paul's, Ashley Down and Montpelier have literally been saved from extinction and at the same time have provided economical housing of reasonable standard. It would be very sad if events in St Pauls in April 1980 led to demands for wholesale rebuilding. The essential fabric of the place is rich and needs to be enhanced through a right balance between old and new.

Renewal is not a new phenomenon, though. It has been usual for city buildings to go through several uses before being replaced. Renewal of this type goes almost totally unnoticed. Who now remembers that King Street, Queen Square, Orchard Street, Great George Street, were once the favoured addresses of Bristol's most well-to-do merchants? On the whole, the grand houses have passed into commercial life rather well, the buildings often remaining dignified whilst serving their new functions amazingly efficiently. New may be a misnomer. Some of these buildings will have been offices for fifty years or more. Only now are fire officers and bye-law officers demanding alterations that threaten their basic domestic character. Renewal or, more accurately, the re-invigoration of degenerating central areas, is mainly concerned with the promotion of new inner city activities that can make use of old buildings and with the idea of people living back in the centre.

The degree of the pressure for change is a significant factor. Too great a financial pressure will tip the scale towards clearance and redevelopment and too little will promote dereliction. The last twenty years have seen both extremes. Many of Bristol's boom office buildings lie on the sites of old buildings that, given the right conditions might have been restored for new uses, while many derelict eighteenth and nineteenth century houses lie on erstwhile office development sites.

Cities are dynamic places that cannot but respond to market

A multiplicity of new uses in King Street. The south side of Brunswick Square still derelict years after its reprieve by the Environment Minister.

forces and social pressures. Planning and conservationist dreams have little hope of realisation unless they recognise and respond to those pressures.

A new appreciation of the qualities of old buildings and a lack of confidence on the part of both designers and lay public have created a positive climate for new buildings within renewal schemes. More and more good new architecture is being created in concert with restoration projects. Architects may well find a new level of confidence through this. Indeed, the regeneration of city centres by means of small scale new work interwoven with the old may be the natural organic way forward for city development.

Urban renewal as a concept is not particularly 'conservative' or resistant to change. At its best, it is – or should be – a means of creating change by evolution.

Because of advances in building technology in the last two generations, few traditional skills remain in the building industry and old, natural materials are rarely used. Consequently, the demolition of a stone building or one built solidly in hand-made bricks is an absolute loss – now virtually irreplaceable. The conservation of buildings even from fifty or sixty years ago therefore assumes even greater significance; a significance further underlined by the energy-conserving qualities of many old buildings.

Ideally, urban renewal schemes should aim not only to give new life to groups of buildings but also to attempt to regenerate complete areas of cities. Since the war, Bristol City Council's concern with the inner city areas on the east and south of the City had been limited to a policy of clearance, with redevelopment of the areas which remained after the motorway needs for land had been satisfied. This policy persisted even into the 1970s, so that much of Easton was developed as high rise flats and initially 'Area D', in St. Paul's, the triangle of land between Ashley and City Road, was cleared of its ninety-seven mostly three- and four-storey Victorian houses. Due to a poor planning brief and dismal architectural treatment, the redevelopment, consisting mostly of one-bedroomed flats in two large blocks, is an affront to the area. The cost of building alone, without the land acquisition costs, worked out at £9,000 per bedroom in 1975/76.

But at least the mistake was recognised. The Joint Committee which dealt with St. Paul's adopted a rehabilitation programme, involving the designation of Housing Action Areas, for the neighbourhood. Grant aid (ranging from 75–90 per cent) became available for basic improvements to private houses, and housing associations and the City Council were able to acquire and rehabilitate tenanted properties.

Following the very successful work achieved in most of the area adjoining City Road, the first Housing Action Area has recently become a General Improvement Area, eligible for 60 per cent grant to carry out general environmental improvements – for example, tree planting, traffic management and organisation of rear access, particularly to provide for car parking. Housing Action Areas have been extended now into Lower Montpelier and Easton.

Bedminster and Totterdown have had an especially raw deal from post war planners. Over five hundred houses and shops were demolished in Totterdown before the second and third stages of the Outer Circuit Road were approved in detail. The remaining houses lost value, but now a Housing Action Area has been established and the area is being upgraded with the help of a Local Plan. In Redcliffe, the eighteenth century development behind St. Mary Redcliffe was cleared, and multi-storey flats were built to take displaced residents both from the Somerset Square and Guinea Street neighbourhood and from the densely populated area on the other side of The Cut, which was to become an industrial estate. The Redcliffe flats have proved to be among the most successful high level dwellings of the period. They seem to have been free of costly structural problems and have worked because people were kept in their own neighbourhood.

However, the cleared area behind and including the once fasionable York Road lay derelict for more than two decades, blighted by road and redevelopment plans and mostly derelict still. On the other side of Bedminster Bridge the situation is similar, with derelict land and empty cottages in New Charlotte Street. In most other cities the New Cut frontage would be recognised for its townscape value and as a splendid example of nineteenth century development. Perhaps that will come now that part has been included in the City Docks Conservation Area. What is interesting from the experience of rehabilitation in

King's Weston: a police HQ and a public open space?

Housing Action Areas is that though the City Council rehabilitates to a higher standard than housing associations (and charge lower rents), rehabilitation tends to be considerably cheaper than new houses on green field sites, when the cost of providing services and infrastructure is taken into account. Rehabilitation in St. Paul's not only costs less than the dismal Area D development, but provides far more attractive accommodation.

However, it must be said that where property has been allowed to rot for decades, rehabilitation becomes similar in cost to new building. The figures for a housing association development in Lodge Street which involves restoration of several derelict Georgian houses and some new flats, works out at £30 per square foot for the restoration and £25 per square foot for the new building. The difference is more than made up by Historic Buildings Council grants available for the restoration of the outer shell of the old buildings, which will make a delightful contribution to the street scene, and VAT means that the government will get some of its money back. But the situation highlights the need for action to be taken so that vacant buildings are repaired quickly and brought back into use rather than for decades to elapse before action is taken. The further recent delay may well prove to be disastrous for the future of this scheme.

In the promotion of Housing Action Areas, a good social mix should be encouraged. The co-operation of socially conscious building societies, too, is necessary, so that owner occupation is not discouraged.

The renewal of the City Docks and the new housing projects there have been discussed separately, for this is to be Bristol's biggest and most exciting revived area. In King Street, old buildings have been restored and the main activities of the area have been altered dramatically from its previous docks, marketing and its earlier mercantile/residential uses. New buildings in the street are not all that special but they do fit unobtrusively amongst the very good collection of old buildings. Perhaps the mix of uses is a little 'fragile' with too many clubs, pubs and restaurants. More residential accommodation to give the elderly residents in the beautiful ancient almshouses some neighbours and a little retail shopping would help.

The much acclaimed pedestrianisation in Corn Street adds dignity to John Wood's great Exchange building.

Important 17th century timber-framed houses in Old Market Street still awaiting restoration.

113

Ashley Road: fine houses are not limited to the city's fashionable suburbs.

Urban Renewal

The Corn Street business area provides an example of an entirely specialist renewal scheme that is now very successful, too. At the height of the office boom, there was a distinct risk that the banks and insurance companies would want to redevelop their Victorian headquarters buildings, or, alternatively, move off to office towers elsewhere, leaving the old business centre underused or even derelict. In a very sensitive operation, planning pressures were brought to bear which have resulted in careful new developments and building rehabilitation 'stitched in' to the existing fabric of this immensely important area of the City.

There are still great opportunities for urban renewal and for housing. Totterdown lies mutilated but alive and kicking in spite of all that has been done to it. Like Kingsdown before it, this is a magnificent hill site just demanding imaginative treatment to convert it back into a marvellous place to live. The most important thing about Totterdown is that, in spite of all, it still has a lively community, ready and anxious to stay on. The same is true of areas like Bedminster and Southville. Here, little or no change has occurred over a long time. There was no heavy war damage, nor has there been much in the way of planning blight to disturb the character of the area. There are problems, though, in what was once the biggest one-class enclave in the City. The industrial heart has gone, with Wills, out to Hartcliffe.

The biggest potential for change through urban renewal in Bristol lies in two areas of commercial building. One of these, Broadmead, may not seem to be an obvious site for development. It is now mostly more than twenty-five years old and still a monument to Bristol's worst architectural era. It needs rejuvenating, as it always did, with a wider range of uses. The floors above many of the shops are grossly underused. Selective redevelopment, the injection of residential accommodation, the forging of new links with Castle Park and, perhaps some architectural 'plastic surgery' to give the place a facelift (like the ill-fated proposal to roof over the pedestrian streets) could result in a dramatic resurgence of Bristol's main shopping centre.

The second area is more important, however. Old Market Street in its pre-war heyday was a lively, coarser place than Castle Street but acting as an extension of it. It had a rich mix of activities with two theatres, a cinema, a great meeting hall and a drill hall; wholesale food, housing, pubs of course – lots of them, as well as the shops. Much of this activity was housed in ancient buildings. Slum clearance after the war in the area to the east of the street, the destruction and replacement of Castle Street and the great gash of the Inner Circuit Road sent it into a thirty year decline. The ancient timber-framed houses on the north have been saved from destruction through a massive and efficient campaign by the amenity societies, but the area is as good as dead. The dereliction seems to be total. At last detailed schemes have been prepared which could bring Old Market Street back to life. Government and commerce together will save it. There seems little doubt now, but it was, as Wellington said, 'a damned close run thing'.

In May 1980 virtually all the city centre urban renewal schemes here including W.C.A., Brunswick Square, Lodge Street and others have been thrown into disarray by precipitate action in response to government economy measures. The amenity societies are at battle stations, intent on a major campaign to reverse the decisions, but the situation seems very grim.

Postscript: Future Bristol

Looking ahead we must admit that the dreams of post war Bristol are going to take much longer to realise than many of us had hoped.

It's hardly surprising. After Hitler's bombs had left such havoc we did not imagine that the developers' bulldozers would also leave so many scars on the face of our City.

I say 'our City' with affection because I believe that many have as great, if not greater, a concern for Bristol as the citizens who were born and bred here. This is all to the City's advantage: with new generations tending to think that their elders have not made such a good job of winning the peace, I am confident amenity societies will continue to exert a powerful influence on our decision-makers. These voluntary bodies, if they speak authoritatively after researching their campaigns, can be valuable watchdogs and earn the respect of both planners and politicians whose attitude of 'we are always right' has now changed for the better.

A local newspaper is close to the grassroots of the communities. It tries to serve and is, therefore, in a special position to feel the pulse and detect the trends. We can therefore expect the *Bristol Evening Post* not only to express opinions, hopefully in a reasoned manner, but to offer a forum to others. Not only do we want to hear the experts. That's a lesson we have learned gradually, particularly in the sixties and seventies. It is the voice of ordinary people that matters – for it is they who have to live with what planners permit.

But all is not lost. Bristol is changing with the times and if we take more care it can remain appealing. Its distinct character must be preserved. No other city is quite like Bristol. Planning must be sensitive and with a realisation that architecture is as much about people as places. One without the other creates conflict.

This is beginning to be appreciated. No longer do modern buildings stick out like the proverbial sore thumb; a number are blending into their surroundings and are pleasant to the eye. We have at the same time to guard our precious landscape, which is why we must encourage the growth of trees and flowers to lend colour to our daily lives.

We have to make sure that the inner city wastelands in the eighties are brought to life again, but not as concrete jungles. More attention should be paid to new housing estates to ensure a sense of lively unity rather than drab uniformity.

Bristol's major task in this decade, however, is to come to terms with the motor car. It must be our servant, not our master. A major debate can be anticipated on the future of public transport; the bus must come into its own again – even if it means a subsidy – and possibly we shall see some form of Metro. Far too many roads, to accommodate more and more cars, have either cut in two or, in some cases, destroyed suburbs. The social damage has been immense, apart from the economics.

We cannot allow this to go on for I fear we shall damage the fabric of the City beyond repair.

Its heart must throb with life.

The City Docks offer a great opportunity to restore, in an imaginative manner, what can become a great attraction, to both local citizens and tourists whom we shall see in greater numbers. Bristol must get on with the development and not flinch from doing so by forming a partnership between the City Council and private enterprise. The empty dockland must be planned so that it is alive with people by day and night – a mix of amenities, homes, offices and shops, as well as boats. It must not become a dead centre – the mistake made with Broadmead where, once the shops close, the streets are deserted.

The future pattern of shopping may well dictate – before the end of the decade – a fresh look at Broadmead. Its role, I feel, could change if more out of town centres are established.

There is much for the watchdogs to observe and to influence; perhaps the greatest challenge facing them is to ensure that Bristol will grow without damaging its environment. A great City at the hub of a motorway complex is bound to boom, attracting more commerce and industries of high technology.

But their offices and factories must fit in so that they do not detract from the skyline or make this a dreary place in which to live and work – as well as play.

Welcome them we must, but with due caution making sure the quality of life is maintained and, if possible, enhanced. Surely that's the prime aim of any amenity society and with this I heartily concur.

Gordon Farnsworth,
Editor, Bristol Evening Post   **May 1980**

Acknowledgements

John Trelawny-Ross for his splendid photographs and for speed and efficiency in producing them. Most of the photographs are by him.

The City of Bristol Planning Office and particularly the Design Section for their help and for photographs.

Derek Balmer for the photograph on page 44 (bottom), Bristol Visual & Environmental Group for the photographs on page 48 and Reece Winstone for those on pages 14, 23, 29 and 30.

Bryan Little for information about the early work of the Bristol amenity societies.

Daphne Turner for information about the development of sports facilities in Bristol.

David Hockin for photography.

Margaret Battson and Anne Mallitte for typing.

The authors for almost meeting our deadlines.

For further reading

The City and County of Bristol — *Bryan Little* / Werner Laurie

Bristol as it was (series) — *Reece Winstone*

Bristol and How it Grew — *Dorothy Brown*

Just Look at Bristol — Bristol Visual and Environmental Group

Bristol, an Architectural History — *Little, Jenner, Gomme* / Lund Humphries

Bristol. (City Buildings series) — *Tom Burrough* / Studio Vista

Georgian Buildings of Bristol — *Walter Ison* / Faber

Victorian Buildings in Bristol — *Clare Crick* / The Redcliffe Press

Changing Bristol: new architecture and conservation 1960–1980 — *Tony Aldous* / The Redcliffe Press

Bristol. Development Plan Review — *J. B. Bennett*

City Centre Policy Report — City & County of Bristol

Bristol City Docks, Consultants' Report — *Casson, Condor & Partners* / City & County of Bristol

Bristol City Docks and its Waterways — *Bristol Planning Group* (OP)

Bristol City Docks Group Reports 1-7 — *Bristol City Docks Group*

Bristol. The Opportunities of the Docks — *J. Preston* / The City of Bristol

The City Docks Draft Local Plan — *I. Patterson* / The City of Bristol

Land Use and Transportation Study (LUTS) Bristol — *Jamieson & Mackay* / City & County of Bristol & Avon County

Changes in the Face of Bristol — *Reece Winstone* (cyclostyled)

Goodbye Britain — *Tony Aldous* / Sidgwick & Jackson

The Rape of Britain — *Amery & Cruikshank* / Elek

120

Notes on contributors

DOROTHY BROWN was recently described in the *Civic Trust News* as one of the Boadiceas of the amenity movement. A graduate of Edinburgh University, born on the Scottish Borders, she was unprepared for the unsung wealth of historic buildings to be found in this part of the West Country. Finding that many buildings were threatened with demolition, she formed the Bristol Visual & Environmental Group to defend Bristol's character. National press and TV publicity highlighted the Group's battles for St. Michael's Hill and Whiteladies Road. Books like *Bristol & How It Grew* and recently *Avon Heritage – the North* have been published to achieve wider recognition of the outstanding number and quality of old buildings in the area. Current concern is with erosion of quality caused by insensitive modernisation of historic buildings and with the wider implications of planning and transport policies.

PATRICK BROWN was born between the wars, and brought up in the heart of the Berkshire countryside. He had an architectural education at the Canterbury School of Architecture and taught there from 1951 when he was a partner in Robert Paine and Partners. He gained experience of small works in the ancient town and the Kentish countryside; he was a founder member of The Canterbury Society, and one time Secretary.

He left Canterbury for Bristol in January 1966, joining Bristol University as lecturer in architecture. He continued his extra-mural lecturing activities and his connection with amenity societies (he was consultant and Expert Witness to the Shepton Mallet Society from 1968 to 1969); he was Treasurer of the Bristol Civic Society from 1966 to 1970; and Chairman from 1971 to 1973. In 1972/74 he was awarded a Fellowship for a study of Redundant Church Re-use, which is now an unpublished thesis. In 1968 he became a member of the Bristol Diocesan Advisory Committee for the care of churches, and also of the Bishop's

Commission on Bristol Historic Churches. He gained an MLitt at Bristol in 1975. He is adviser to several churches in Bristol Diocese (Quinquennial review architect), and recently completed a major re-ordering of the medieval church at Yate.

His publications include the booklet *Eight Bristol Churches* and articles on conservation and re-use of redundant churches in the *Architectural Review*.

He is married, with two sons, one reading architecture, the other approaching 'A' levels. His enthusiasm are travel – especially in Europe, Baroque design, music of the Romantic era, buying books and the study of small towns.

PAMELA COBB, a graduate of Edinburgh University, worked in adult education at Leeds and with the Open University before coming to Bristol University in 1973. Involvement in environmental matters began with an amateur interest in architecture and developed into a deep concern for canals and canalside buildings.

Member of the Inland Waterways Amenity Advisory Council set up under the 1968 Transport Act, and chairman of the Inland Waterways Association North East Branch and its representative on the national Council. Concern for canalside improvements including landscaping in Leeds city centre led to more general activity with Leeds Civic Trust.

On moving to Bristol, decided that involvement with the Civic Society and Bristol City Docks Group would be the best way to learn about and identify with her new environment.

RICHARD FLOWERDEW is a 31-year-old solicitor who lives in a Victorian house in Clifton. Married, with two young children, he is a determined town-dweller and has lived in Bristol for sixteen years. He has for several years been convenor of the Civic Society's Projects Group, which looks at and comments on planning applications, and he is Civic Society representative on and Chairman of the City's Conservation Advisory Panel. He has frequently presented the amenity society case at public inquiries.

PETER FLOYD is a member of the Royal Town Planning Institute and an Associate of the Royal Institute of British Architects.

He holds the Diploma of the RWA School of Architecture and the Diploma in Civic Design of the University of Edinburgh.

From 1955–62 he worked for private practices in Bristol and London and from 1964 until 1966 in the Bristol Planning Department where he was a member of the team which produced the City Centre Policy Report. He then spent a year as a lecturer in the School of Architecture in the University of Hong Kong. In 1967 he rejoined Bristol Planning Department and for two years was seconded to the Severnside Physical Planning Unit.

He returned to become deputy head of the Design Section, becoming head in 1970. In 1972 he joined Moxley Jenner and Partners.

He has devised and run planning courses for architectural students at Bath University, for planning students at Bristol Polytechnic and for architectural students at Hong Kong University.

He has served on the Council of the Bristol Society of Architects, the Avon County Committee of the Council for the Protection of Rural England and is past Chairman of the Bristol Civic Society. He is currently Senior Vice Chairman of the Royal Town Planning Institute, South West Branch.

ANNE and JERRY HICKS married and settled in Bristol in 1952. Since then they have lived close to the City Centre and raised two children. Both were trained at the Slade School of Art and have combined professional painting with teaching; Anne works part time with adults including the University Department of Architecture, and Jerry is Head of Art at Cotham Grammar School. They are members of the Royal West of England Academy and have exhibited work widely in Britain and abroad though mainly in the West Country. Anne has represented British women painters in Paris, and Jerry won the Queen's Jubilee Award for painting British Achievements in Sport and the Bristol 600 painting award. Collaboration has included public murals in Bristol and theatre design.

Jerry (4th Dan Judo Black Belt) was a founder member of the Bristol, Avon and South West Sports Councils, the Bristol Arts Consultative Committee, and the Friends of the s.s. *Great Britain.*

In a period of desperation he also invented 'Dodo'. Their environmental activities have been mainly on a personal basis, but they helped form the Bristol City Docks Group for which they compiled Report No. 7.

DAVID HIRSCHMANN came to Bristol as a student in 1957. Became a lecturer in the Department of Philosophy of the University of Bristol in 1964.

His wife started the Bristol branch of Shelter in 1968 and between then and 1973 he helped to run this and the St. Paul's Housing Advisory Service. He acted as co-ordinator of the Outer Circuit Road Campaign. Has two children.

GORDON PRIEST, a Bristolian, is Chairman of the Bristol Civic Society and has served on its committee for some years; he is a past Chairman of the Friends of Bristol Art Gallery and has been Treasurer of the Bristol Society of Architects.

He is a lecturer in architecture at the University of Bristol. Has worked in Canada and was in architectural partnership in Bristol. Currently working on a documentary study of the Exchange in Bristol. Has been involved in many of the local conservation battles described here. Married with a daughter. Enjoys beachcombing, painting, writing and is no longer able to afford the compulsive collecting of delftware, English watercolours and Bristol topographical prints.

REECE WINSTONE born and educated in Bristol, spent the first part of his working life in his father's menswear business where he gained 'a first class education in salesmanship and display'.

His interest and hobby of photography started in 1924 when he was 15, but by then he was already involved in local history. He became a professional photographer before the war.

He published the first of the *Bristol as it was* series in 1957. The thirtieth is coming out in 1980.

He is an ex-chairman of Bristol Civic Society and its first Honorary Life Member, and is a fellow of the Royal Photographic Society and past president of the Western Counties Photographic Federation.

INDEX